the
homemade home
for children

the
homemade home
for children

50 thrifty and chic projects for creative parents

Sania Pell

CICO BOOKS
LONDON NEW YORK

This book is dedicated to my family, with love to you all.

Published in 2012 by CICO Books
an imprint of Ryland Peters & Small
519 Broadway, 5th Floor, New York NY 10012
20–21 Jockey's Fields, London WC1R 4BW

www.cicobooks.com

10 9 8 7 6 5 4 3 2 1

ISBN: 978 1 908170 19 4

Printed in China

Project editor: Gillian Haslam
Editor: Alison Wormleighton
Design: Elizabeth Healey
Photography: Emma Lee
Illustration: Trina Dalziel

Contents

Introduction

Life changes when you have children, and so does your home, offering a fantastic opportunity to make things your children will love to use. Not only are the projects in the book stylish enough that they can be left out on show, but they will inspire you and your family to be imaginative and playful while enjoying making them.

This book is not just for parents and children—grandparents, friends, and teachers will also find it useful, as many projects make ideal gifts. Some ideas are decorative, others are practical, some are simply fun, and many have an educational slant. The projects cost next to nothing because they are made from materials like fabric remnants, flea-market finds, leftover paint, and items from nature. There is something for all levels of ability, and you can follow every step or simply use the ideas as starting points.

Children can be involved right from the beginning. If you incorporate their ideas so that the projects reflect their personalities, they will enjoy the results even more. If they are old enough, involve them in making the projects (under supervision). It will help develop their skills, from drawing, coloring, and painting to cutting out or sewing. I fondly remember creating things as a child, and now my children love to do the same. I can tell how proud they are when we hang their drawings on the wall or give their homemade gifts to family or friends. I have drawn upon my experience as a designer, a stylist, a maker, and a mother to come up with the ideas in this book. I hope it inspires you and sparks your children's imagination. Make the projects with love and laughter, and give or display them with pride and joy—these are the ingredients I believe help make a happy family home.

Sania Pell

CHAPTER 1 # Nursery

Create a cheerful, cozy, and stimulating environment for a baby with the projects in this chapter. They range from a soft, cuddly blanket and a charming table lamp to decorative items to hang on the walls or from the ceiling where they will catch the baby's eye and provide hours of interest. Some, like the hand prints, are so sweet that you'll want to keep them as mementoes forever.

Baby
blanket

A baby blanket makes a practical and beautiful gift, for a friend's baby or your own. This blanket is made from wool felted in the washing machine to soften it. It has raised shapes to add more textural interest, and when the baby is older the shapes will be a delight to feel and play with. Try to keep the stitching looking neat from the back, too—if necessary, you could attach a soft backing to cover them up. To launder the blanket, hand wash in cool water. The instructions are for the colors I used but you can change them if you prefer, for example to traditional pink or blue for a baby girl or boy.

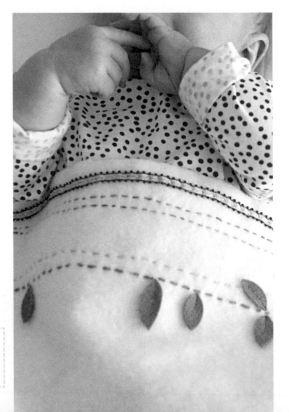

materials and equipment

24 x 32in (60 x 80cm) and 12 x 10in (30 x 25cm) rectangles of soft wool or wool mix in cream

12 x 10in (30 x 25cm) rectangle of soft wool or wool mix in gray

Washing machine and detergent for sensitive skin

Small, sharp scissors and pins

Sewing needle and thread in cream and gray

Tailor's chalk and long ruler

Embroidery needle and stranded floss in gray, red, cream, and light gray

Sewing machine with embroidery foot

Scrap of suede in pale yellow

Patterns for two birds (see page 185)

About 22in (56cm) of red/cream ribbon

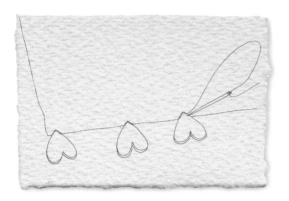

1 To felt the cream and gray wool, wash the three rectangles in the washing machine at 140°F (60°C) using a detergent for sensitive skin. While still damp, pull them into shape and leave to dry flat. My larger rectangle of cream wool shrank by about a quarter, to 18 x 24½in (45 x 62cm). From the smaller cream rectangle, cut out eight hearts. Using a double length of cream thread, hand sew them very securely to the bottom short edge of the larger cream rectangle. (This is important to prevent small pieces being pulled off by the baby and swallowed.)

2 Using tailor's chalk and a long ruler, draw a line about 1in (2.5cm) from the bottom edge and parallel to it. With three strands of gray floss, embroider running stitch along the line. Cut out 19 small leaves from the gray rectangle. Pin them at equal intervals along the embroidered line, so that they are alternately above and below the line. With a double length of gray thread, hand sew each leaf in place very securely at one end; remove the pins.

3 Draw lines 2¼in (6cm), 2½in (6.5cm), 3¼in (8.5cm), and 5in (13cm) from the bottom edge. With three strands of red floss, embroider running stitch along the lower three of these lines. Now embroider the upper line with six strands of gray floss, again using running stitch. (Often you can do three or four stitches before pulling the needle and thread through, as shown, speeding up the process.)

4 Cut out eight gray leaves and one gray heart. Pin these above or below the line of gray running stitch. Using a double length of cream thread (for contrast), hand sew the leaves and heart in position—I used running stitch along the length of the outer leaves. Remove the pins. Using three strands of red floss, embroider an intermittent line of cross stitches, as shown, about ¼in (5mm) above the gray running stitch.

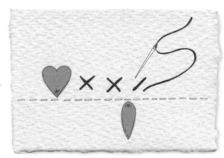

5 Draw a line 8in (20cm) from the lower edge of the blanket. Cut out nine cream leaves, pinning them at equal intervals along the marked line, alternately above and below it. Thread the sewing machine with gray thread on both the top and the bobbin, fit the embroidery foot, and set the machine to darning and free-moving. Machine embroider along the marked line, and when you reach a leaf, remove the pin and make a "detour" to stitch up or down the center of the leaf and back again, before continuing along the marked line. Also occasionally machine embroider a leaf shape without using a felted wool leaf. Finish by cutting out a suede leaf and sewing it on by hand with running stitch down the center.

6 Draw lines 10in (25cm) and 10½in (27cm) from the bottom edge. Using six strands of red floss, embroider running stitch along the upper line, and French knots (see Needle Case, step 4, page 100) along the line beneath it. Using the bird patterns, cut out a bird facing left, another facing right (using the same pattern but in reverse), and two seen from the back, all from the gray felted wool. Using tiny running stitches in gray thread, hand sew them in place sitting on the upper line.

7 Draw lines 1in (2.5cm), 1¼in (3cm), 2¾in (7cm), and 3¼in (8.5cm) from the top edge. Embroider these in running stitch using three strands of red floss for the top two lines, three strands of light gray floss for the third line down, and six strands of gray floss for the fourth line down. Cut out three suede and six gray leaves and hand sew them above or below the gray line using small running stitches down the middle of each leaf in matching thread.

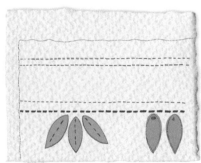

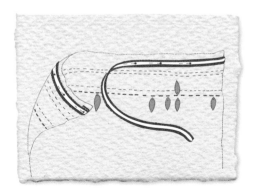

8 Turn under one end of the ribbon and pin it ⅜in (1cm) from the top edge on the back of the blanket, starting at one side. Bring the ribbon around the other side edge to the front. Pin in place, removing the pins on the back and replacing them with the ones on the front, so that you have pinned the two ribbons together with the felted wool sandwiched between them. When you reach the side edge at which you started, trim off the excess ribbon and turn under the end. Hand sew through all layers with running stitch in matching thread; remove pins.

13

Pompom
rabbit picture

Brighten up a corner of the nursery with a charming picture of a rabbit with a fluffy pompom tail. It is simple to make from a small stretched canvas, which you first paint and then decorate with fabric appliqué and embroidery. For the rabbit, choose a fabric with splashes of color to catch the baby's attention—here a floral fabric is used for the rabbit shape and also to provide flowers that can be cut out and attached to the canvas. The design can be either simple or complex: just one simple, bold flower plus hand embroidery, or a lot of flowers with both hand and machine embroidery. But be warned—making pompoms is addictive, and you may find yourself applying them to the edges of blankets and pillows as well!

materials and equipment

Canvas stretched on a frame—my two canvases were 12 x 10in (30 x 25cm) and 7 x 7in (18 x 18cm)

Latex (emulsion) paint in neutral color such as off-white or gray

½in (1.5cm) flat brush

Iron, ironing board, and press cloth

Fusible web

Patterned fabric such as floral fabric

Pins

Small, sharp scissors and general-purpose scissors

Pattern for rabbit (see page 186)

Pattern for flower (optional—see page 187)

Pencil

Pictures of flowers, for reference (optional)

Sewing machine with embroidery foot, plus dark thread (for machine-embroidered picture)

Embroidery needle and floss in a dark shade

Cardboard (an old cereal box works well)

Compass

Yarn, for pompom tail

Sewing needle and thread to match floral fabric

Machine-embroidered picture

1 Paint the right side of the stretched canvas with latex (emulsion) paint using a flat brush. Allow to dry and then apply a second coat.

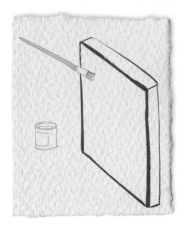

2 While the paint is drying, iron fusible web to the wrong side of the fabric, following the manufacturer's instructions. Pin the rabbit pattern to the fabric, paying attention to where you position it on the floral pattern, and cut it out with small scissors. Also cut out some flower heads and leaves from this fabric. If you aren't using a floral fabric, cut out flower shapes using the flower pattern on page 187.

3 Turn over the canvas when it is completely dry and draw stems, along with additional flowers and leaves, on the wrong side of the canvas with a pencil, using pictures of flowers as reference if you wish. Remember that this design is the reverse of what will actually appear on the front. Thread the sewing machine with a dark thread, and remove the embroidery foot and needle so you can slide the canvas underneath. It should be upside down, so you can see the drawing. Fit the needle and embroidery foot, and set the machine to darning or free-flowing. Machine embroider the design you have drawn. Remove the foot and needle again, and slide the canvas out.

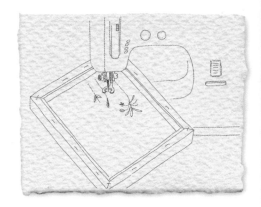

4 With the canvas right side up, hand embroider a line parallel to the bottom edge of the canvas in running stitch using an embroidery needle and dark floss. Also hand embroider a running stitch stem for the right-hand flower. Remove the backing paper from the rabbit and position it on the canvas. Cover with a cloth to prevent the iron from touching the painted canvas directly, and iron in place. Repeat to attach the flower heads and cut-out leaves to the stems. Turn the canvas over and, if possible, iron the back of the canvas to ensure the pieces are secure.

5 For the pompom, draw two 1¾in (4.5cm) circles of cardboard using a compass and pencil. Cut out with general-purpose shears. Cut out a ¾in (2cm) hole from the center of each, and cut a slit in each, widening the outer part of the slit. Place the two circles on

top of each other and wrap the yarn around them, covering the end you've started with to hold it in place. The slit makes the winding process quicker than if you had to insert the end through the ever-decreasing central hole each time. Continue wrapping closely until you have gone around the ring at least twice. The more yarn you use, the tighter the pompom will be.

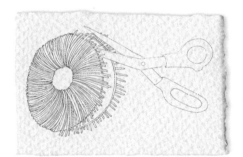

6 Now slip the scissors blade between the two layers of cardboard and cut through the yarn, gradually working all the way around the circumference.

7 Cut a 12in (30cm) piece of yarn and wind it around the center, between the two cardboard rings. Knot it tightly, then wrap the piece of yarn around to the other side and knot it tightly again. Slide the cardboard rings off and trim the outside of the pompom if there are any stray bits of yarn sticking out. Attach the pompom to the rabbit as a tail by sewing it to the canvas with a needle and thread.

Hand-embroidered picture

Make this as for the machine-embroidered picture, but in step 2 cut out one large flower head and one large leaf from the fabric, omit step 3, and in step 4 embroider a vertical stem near the left side, rather than the horizontal line for the ground and the stem on the right.

Bowl of goldfish
mobile

Hang this pretty mobile high above a crib so that the baby can watch the two colorful goldfish "swim" in their bowl and enjoy the reflections from the moving crystal "bubbles." A bent coat hanger with some extra wire attached is simply covered with several different fabrics, some patterned and some solid-color, in watery blue-green shades. The pair of goldfish, which hang by threads so that they appear to be swimming, are made from two colorful fine lawn fabrics in exotic patterns. The vintage crystal droplets also hang from threads, to resemble bubbles moving up to the water's surface.

materials and equipment

Wire coat hanger

39in (1m) length of wire finer than coat hanger

Seven lengths of fabric, each ¾ x 16in (2 x 40cm), in shades of blue-green (you can use shorter strips but you will need more of them)

Iron and ironing board

Double-sided tape

Patterns for fish (see page 189)

Scraps of two print fabrics in bright colors such as red or orange, for fish

Pins and small, sharp scissors

Sewing machine and thread to match fish fabric

Batting (wadding)

Pencil

Sewing needle and white thread

Embroidery needle and floss in black

Four crystal chandelier droplets

About ten small glass beads

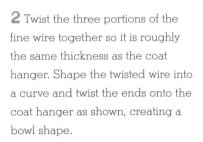

2 Twist the three portions of the fine wire together so it is roughly the same thickness as the coat hanger. Shape the twisted wire into a curve and twist the ends onto the coat hanger as shown, creating a bowl shape.

1 Bend the coat hanger into an oval shape, gently easing out any kinks with your hands. Take the fine wire and bend it into thirds.

3 To bind the wire with the blue-green strips, first turn under and press ¼in (5mm) on one long edge and both ends of each strip. Stick a ¾in (2cm) piece of double-sided tape to the coat hanger at the end of the hook, and remove the backing paper. Stick one end of a fabric strip to the tape and begin spiraling the strip around the coat hanger as shown, so that the turned-under edge of the new round covers the raw edge of the previous round. When you get to the end of the strip, stick it in place with a piece of tape. Start a new strip as before, and continue in this way till all the wire is covered.

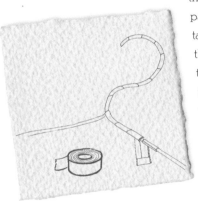

4 To make the fish, fold one of the bright fabric scraps in half and pin the body pattern to the double layer. Cut around the pattern so you have two fish body shapes, and pin these with right sides together. Using matching threads, machine stitch a ⅛in (3mm) seam around the edges, leaving the tail open. Repeat to create a second fish.

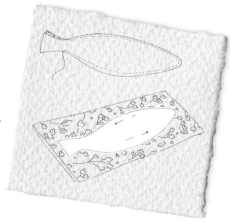

5 Turn the two fish right side out, press, and stuff each with batting (wadding) through the tail. (You will need to stuff just a small amount at a time, pushing it in with a pencil if necessary.)

6 Using the pattern, cut out two fins and one tail for each fish from the other print fabric. With a needle and matching thread, sew running stitch across the short end of each piece, knotting one end of the thread and leaving the other end long. Pull the thread to gather the fabric tightly on each; knot the other end.

7 Insert the gathered end of one tail into the opening in one stuffed fish, and turn under the raw edges of the opening. Hand sew in place over the tail. Sew a gathered-up fin to each side of the fish. Using an embroidery needle and black floss, embroider an eye in satin stitch (see Needle Case, step 2, page 100) on each side of the fish. Repeat this step for the other fish.

8 With a sewing needle, attach white thread to the top of one fish with several small stitches. Leaving a 2in (5cm) length of thread, sew the other end into the fabric-covered curved wire that forms the top of the "goldfish bowl"; finish with a knot. Repeat for the other fish, leaving a 4in (10cm) length of thread this time. With the same needle and the white thread, make some stitches in the fabric covering the wire, then take the thread through the holes in a crystal droplet and two or three glass beads, and make more stitches and a knot in the fabric. Adjust the heights at which these "bubbles" hang. Hang the mobile well out of reach of the baby.

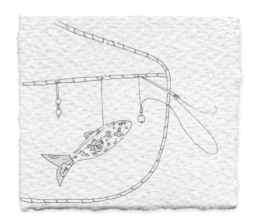

Butterfly
table lamp

It's surprising how easy it is to transform a plain lamp into something personal for a child, using only a few pieces of fabric, a handful of buttons, and a little stitching. This table lamp can begin in the nursery and then **more detail can be added as the child grows older**, so that they can be involved and can help with the process—the lamp can grow with them. Match the fabric you use to material used elsewhere in the room, or use leftovers from a homemade dress. Paint the lamp to coordinate with the fabric colors, and add ribbon in a similar shade around the base to finish it off.

materials and equipment

Lamp with cream shade

Pattern for butterly (see page 188), or an illustration or computer printout of butterfly, for reference

Tracing paper (or greaseproof paper) and pencil

Masking tape

Sewing needle and cream thread

Embroidery needle and stranded floss in a dark color

Small, sharp scissors

Scrap of fabric with individual flower motifs suitable for cutting out

Scraps of other fabrics

Five or six buttons in different colors and sizes

Undercoat (optional)

½in (1.5cm) flat paintbrush

Acrylic or water-based eggshell paint to match decoration on shade (I used four colors)

Piece of linen fabric at least as large as bottom of lamp base

White glue

Ribbon (no wider than depth of lamp base)

1 Remove the shade from the lamp. Either use the butterfly pattern or trace an illustration of a butterfly. Use a little masking tape to attach it to the shade. Holding it steady, transfer the butterfly outline to the shade by pricking through the outline and through the lampshade with a sewing needle. Remove the paper.

2 With an embroidery needle and two strands of dark-colored floss, embroider the outline of the butterfly in running stitch, through the holes you made in step 1. Make a French knot (see Needle Case, step 4, page 100) at the end of each of the two antennae. Embroider the line between the top half and the bottom half of each wing using backstitch. (To work backstitch, bring the needle out on the line, insert it half a stitch length behind this on the stitching line, and bring it out half a stitch length ahead of the thread. Repeat, inserting the needle at the end of the previous stitch, and continue in this way along the line.)

3 Cut out individual flowers from floral fabric and sew these to the shade. Some of them can project beyond the edge if you wish. Cut out one or two 1 x 3in (2.5 x 7.5cm) strips from other fabric, wrap them over the lower edge of the shade so that the shade is sandwiched between the two halves, and sew in place using running stitch. You could also cut out smaller fabric strips and sew these in place elsewhere on the shade.

4 Embroider a few leaves and stems in running stitch using an embroidery needle and two strands of dark floss. You could also use satin stitch (see Needle Case, step 2, page 100) for some of the leaves if you wish.

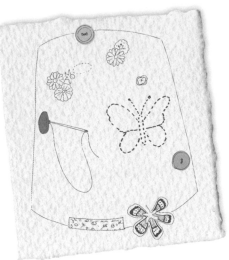

5 Sew five or six buttons to the shade with a sewing needle and thread. They will look best if you concentrate them in clusters with the flowers, so that there are also spaces in between. One or two of these can also project beyond the edge if you wish.

6 Paint the lamp with undercoat using a flat brush, and allow it to dry. (If it is white, you don't need to undercoat it.) Now paint it in colors to match the shade, using different colors in the lamp's different sections.

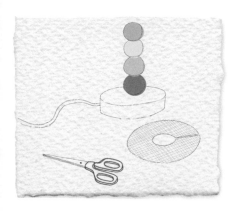

7 With a pencil, draw around the base of the lamp on a piece of linen fabric and cut out the shape. Cut a radius from the outer edge to the center. Measure the thickness of the upright part of the lamp just above the base, draw a circle with a diameter of this size at the center of the fabric circle, and cut out. Apply white glue to the back of the linen, slide the linen onto the top of the base, and glue the linen to it, butting up the edges of the radius.

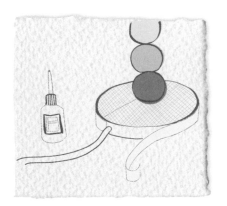

8 Measure the circumference of the base and cut a length of ribbon to this length. Apply glue to the back of the ribbon and glue it to the edge of the lamp base, starting and ending at the electric cord.

Handprint pictures

Make these handprint pictures when your child is still a baby, and hang them on the wall of the nursery. As the child grows up, he or she will adore looking at them and asking, "Was I really that small?" The pictures will make a fabulous wall decoration for years to come. You could even take prints on a regular basis, perhaps making them part of a birthday ritual, and then display them together.

✸ Use a good-quality white watercolor paper with black acrylic paint or the occasional fluorescent paint for an eye-catching pop of color, or use white paint on black paper. For a group of handprints, use a combination of these to create maximum impact.

✸ Load a ½in (1.5cm) flat paintbrush with paint and completely cover the palm of your child's hand with the paint. Turn the child's hand over and press the palm down onto the paper, making sure every finger has some pressure applied, and that the child doesn't wriggle or move their hand at all.

✸ Make several prints at a time, and then frame the best one. You could give extra prints as a gift to grandparents or use them as special thank you cards.

✸ Add your child's age and the date using inked rubber stamps, stencils, or found vintage numerals.

✸ When dry, frame the pictures—box frames look good, particularly if you emphasize the 3D look by slightly raising the print off the backing card using adhesive fixing pads.

Enchanted branch

Hung above the crib or changing mat in the nursery, the delicate lace and felt leaves suspended from this painted branch will dance in the slightest breeze and attract a baby's attention. Sequins and metallic fabric add a little sparkle to catch the light.

✸ Find a thin, dry branch about 1yd (1m) long that has fallen from a tree, and collect a selection of leaves in different sizes and shapes—older children could help with this. Paint the branch with two coats of white latex (emulsion) paint using a ¾in (2cm) brush, allowing the paint to dry after each coat.

✸ Choose a stiff fabric like felt, or iron fusible web to the wrong side of thinner fabric to stiffen it. Pin the real leaves to the fabric and cut out about 50 leaf shapes from the fabric. Unpin and discard the real leaves.

✸ Cut ten 20–40in (50–100cm) lengths of narrow ribbon and lace, and sew the fabric leaves to them using tiny stitches and matching thread. For some, just sew leaves to one end, and for others sew smaller leaves along the length of the ribbon or lace. Sew leaves to both ends of the longest ribbons or lace.

✸ Decorate the leaves by sewing on flower and leaf shapes cut from scraps of vintage lace and/or metallic fabric. Also sew on some sequins, positioning them to hide knots and stitches. Tie the other end of each length of ribbon or lace to the branch, and loop the longer lengths over the branch so that both ends hang down.

✸ Cut a 1yd (1m) length of white ribbon, or adjust the length to suit the spot where you are hanging the branch. Tie both ends to the branch and hang from a hook, making sure it is out of the baby's reach.

QUICK IDEAS
Building blocks

Every toddler enjoys playing with blocks, and it is also the perfect gift for a new baby, especially if presented in a beautiful box. Buy some inexpensive, unpainted wooden cubes—there are lots of sizes available online, but I used 1in (2.5cm) cubes (not suitable for babies) and 1½in (4cm) cubes.

✳ Have fun with colors, using acrylic paints and a ⅜in (1cm) flat brush to paint each side a different shade, and occasionally using metallic gold. Leave to dry.

✳ After painting them, personalize some of the blocks by gluing on cut-out images that you and your child have chosen together. You can find them in many sources, such as old books that have fallen into disrepair, catalogs, and old postcards that you come across at book sales, thrift stores, and garage sales, as well as on the internet. Cut them out and attach them with white glue.

✳ When the blocks are dry, apply a coat of clear, flat water-based varnish.

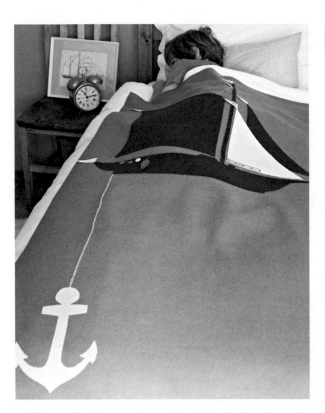

CHAPTER 2 # Bedroom

This chapter includes projects to personalize a child's bedroom so that it reflects their own interests and tastes while still looking stylish and working with the rest of the house. Whether the child is fascinated by nature, by the stars and planets, or by planes and boats, many of these projects—not least the height board—will stay with them as they grow up.

Floral
Wall hanging

Made from a combination of realistic silk flowers and stylized leaves and flower petals cut from fabric, all sewn onto a linen background, this dramatic wall hanging will brighten up a child's bedroom or playroom. Embroidered leaves and stems provide delicate detailing and create the feeling of an enchanted garden. If you involve your child in choosing the flowers, the hanging is destined to become a firm favorite, possibly even a family heirloom and cherished reminder of childhood—especially if the fabric used for the leaves and petals has been cut from an outgrown or worn-out favorite dress belonging to the child.

materials and equipment

Dressmaker's shears and small, sharp scissors

Linen fabric

Tape measure

Pins

Iron and ironing board

Sewing machine (optional)

Sewing needle and matching thread

Fusible web

Scraps of print and solid-color fabric

Silk flowers

Real leaves (optional)

Pencil or tailor's chalk

Embroidery needle and floss

Ribbon (optional)

Two buttons

1 Using dressmaker's shears, cut out the linen fabric to the desired size, if possible with the selvedge running down the sides. Fray the top and bottom edges by using a pin to tease out and remove threads parallel to these edges. If the wall hanging is to be smaller than the fabric width, you could fray all four edges rather than incorporating the selvedges. Or, if you prefer, you could cut the fabric a little bigger all around and then turn under, press, pin, and stitch a hem on each edge.

2 Following the manufacturer's instructions, iron fusible web to the back of the scraps of print and solid-color fabrics. Using small, sharp scissors, cut out simple flower heads, leaves, and stems from the fabrics. (You don't need a stem for every flower head, because some of the stems will be machine embroidered instead.) For more intricate leaf shapes, you could use leaves from the silk flowers or even real leaves as patterns, pinning them to the print or solid-color fabric and cutting around them.

3 Pull the silk flower heads off their stems, and experiment with arrangements of the silk and fabric flower heads and the fabric leaves and stems on the linen. The stems should all finish on the bottom edge of the linen. Once you are happy with the arrangement, pin all the fabric shapes in place. Mark with pencil or tailor's chalk where the silk flowers will go.

4 Following the manufacturer's instructions, remove the backing paper from the fabric shapes and iron in place on the linen.

5 Either machine embroider the remaining stems using a wide zigzag stitch or hand embroider them in running stitch.

6 Hand embroider the detail on the leaves using running stitch and embroidery thread in a darker shade of the leaf color. Also embroider the remaining stems with running stitch along the length.

7 Using thread that matches the flower, hand sew each silk flower in place in several places where the stitches won't show.

8 To make ties by which the wall hanging can be hung, cut two strips of print fabric or two lengths of ribbon, fold them in half crosswise, and sew the folded end of each securely to the front of the linen at the top corners. Sew buttons on top as decorative detail.

Sailboat-at-anchor
bed runner

This decorative bed runner will inspire dreams of sailing to foreign lands and give a focal point to a child's bedroom for many years, as it won't be outgrown quickly. The motif can be as simple or complicated as you like. The boat could be simplified right down to a series of triangles and a long rectangle with the edges cut diagonally for young children, or given extra detail for older children. The pieces of tape measure add a quirky graphic element, as does the oversized anchor. Place the runner down the middle of the bed as in the photograph, or crosswise at the end of the bed with the anchor hanging down to the floor.

materials and equipment

Set square (or large book or magazine)

Tailor's chalk, tape measure, and long ruler

Thick suiting felt in blue-gray and dark blue

Dressmaker's shears and small, sharp scissors

Iron and ironing board

Fusible web

Canvas or felt in off-white

Patterns for boat and anchor (see page 190)

Pins

Button about ⅝in (1.5cm) in diameter

Sewing needle and matching thread

Embroidery needle and stranded embroidery floss in dark gray and cream

Scrap of orange felt, for fender

Old fabric tape measure to cut up

Orange ribbon (optional) —I used 12in (30cm) of ¾in- (2cm-) wide velvet ribbon

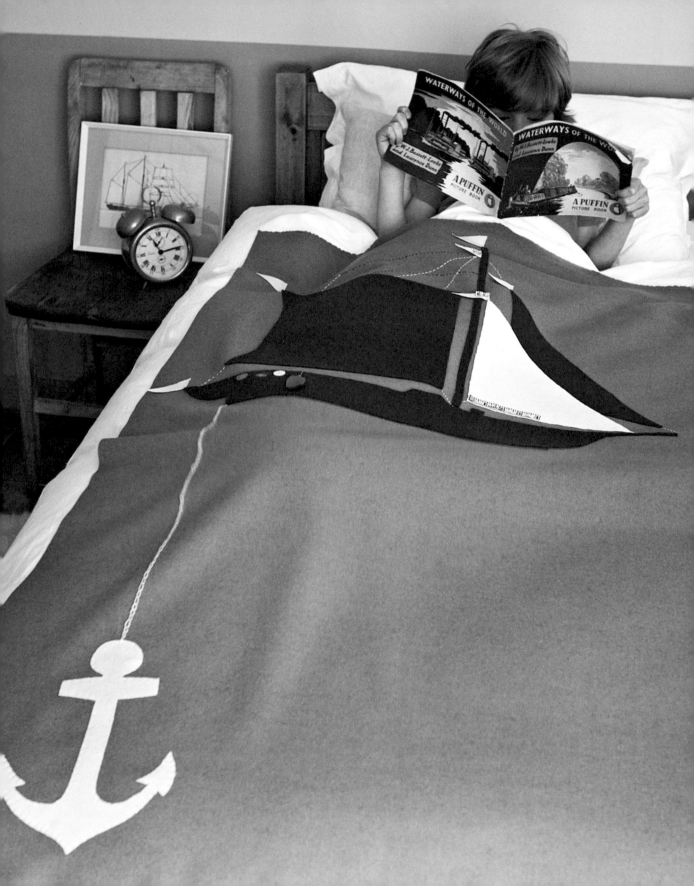

1 Using a set square (or the corner of a magazine or large book), tailor's chalk, tape measure, and long ruler, mark out a 33 x 59in (85 x 150cm) rectangle of blue-gray felt. Cut out with dressmaker's shears. Because felt does not ravel, it doesn't need hemming. Following the manufacturer's instructions, iron fusible web to the back of the dark blue felt and the off-white canvas or felt. Using the pattern pieces, cut out a triangular sail and an anchor from the off-white canvas or felt, and a hull, mast, mainsail, and visible portion of a triangular sail from the dark blue felt.

2 Cut out a porthole in the hull. The easiest way to do this accurately is to draw around the button, ¼in (5mm) from the top edge, and then fold the fabric through the center of the circle, so you can still see half of your drawn circle. Using small, sharp scissors, cut out the semicircle, cutting through both layers, then unfold the felt, revealing a circular hole.

3 Use tailor's chalk to draw a line on the blue-gray rectangle 27½in (70cm) from the top edge and parallel to it. Remove the backing paper from the felt pieces and pin them to the rectangle, fusible side down. Start with the hull, centering it between the side edges and placing its bottom edge on the line you've drawn. Next pin the sails and mast in place, and then the anchor, which should be about 3½in (8.5cm) from the left edge and 5¼in (13.5cm) from the bottom edge of the rectangle. Iron in place, removing the pins as you go.

4 Use a sewing needle and thread that matches each piece to sew running stitch around the edges of all the shapes you've ironed in place.

5 With tailor's chalk and the ruler, draw the lines of the rigging and the anchor chain. Using three strands of floss, embroider them in running stitch with dark gray floss for the horizontal ropes and cream floss for all the other ropes.

6 Embroider the anchor chain in chain stitch using all six strands of cream floss. Chain stitch is worked from top to bottom—bring the needle up from the underside, and insert it again into the same hole or very close to it, leaving a loop. Bring the needle up through the loop, one stitch length farther along the vertical stitching line—my stitches are ⅜in (1cm) long on this project. Insert it again in the same hole or very close to it, again leaving a loop. Continue in this way down the stitching line.

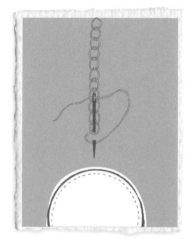

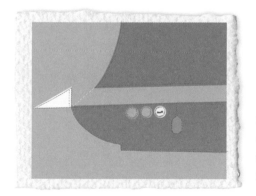

7 From a blue-gray felt scrap, draw around the button and cut out a blue-gray circle for another porthole. Also cut out a ½ x ¾ in (12mm x 2cm) blue-gray felt rectangle, an orange felt fender, and five off-white canvas or felt flags. In matching thread, sew on the fender and porthole as shown, and sew the rectangle in place at the right of the mast, using running stitch around the edges of all three pieces. Sew on the flags along their short edges only, to allow them to flap. Now sew on the button as a third porthole, and embroider a rope for the fender in running stitch using three strands of cream floss.

8 For a graphic touch, cut an old fabric tape measure into a few pieces and sew these to a sail and two flags. And if you wish, you can add a flash of bright color by sewing on a short length of orange ribbon at the bottom edge of the runner.

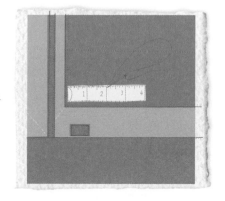

Clay butterfly
garland

The dusky pinks and soft blues of these delicate strings of butterflies add **charm and faded prettiness to any room**, and are ideal for a young girl's bedroom. Because they are made from air-drying clay, they are breakable and should be hung out of reach of little fingers. Drape a string of butterflies over a picture frame, hang several strings of butterflies from nails in rows on the wall, or prop up individual butterflies on a mantelpiece. You could also use different sizes of butterflies, or cut out other shapes, such as flowers or fruit, from the clay and intersperse them with the butterflies.

materials and equipment

Air-drying clay in white

Rolling pin

Butterfly cookie cutter

Buttons (optional)

Chopping board and skewer

Mugs

Emery board or fine sandpaper

Clean cloth and old newspaper

¾in (2cm) flat artist's brush

Latex (emulsion) or acrylic paint in neutral tones

Large-eyed needle and twine or fine ribbon

Small silk flowers

Craft glue (optional)

1 Take a good handful of clay (sealing the pack so that the rest doesn't dry out). On a work surface, roll out the clay with a rolling pin to ⅛in (3mm) thick.

2 Use a butterfly cookie cutter to cut out the shapes. If you want to decorate some of the butterflies with buttons, push the buttons into the shape before removing the cutter from the shape. (The buttons will be glued on later.)

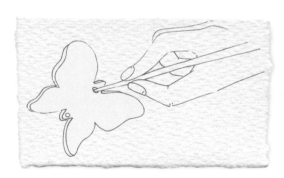

3 After removing the cutter, place the shapes on a chopping board. With a skewer, pierce two holes in each, one near the top and the other near the bottom of the body, while still wet.

4 Place some mugs on their sides and lay one shape over each so they will dry in a curved shape. Leave others on the chopping board to dry flat. The drying process will take about 24 hours.

5 When the clay is dry, sand the edges of the butterflies using an emery board or fine sandpaper. Wipe off any dust with a cloth, then lay the shapes on old newspaper. Using a paintbrush, paint one side of each butterfly. Leave to dry, and then turn each shape over and paint the other side. Repeat until the color is solid.

6 When the paint is dry, thread a needle with twine or fine ribbon a bit longer than the desired length of the garland. Thread it through the holes in one butterfly, starting and finishing at the back. To hold in place, knot the twine or ribbon at the back next to the holes (leaving enough twine or ribbon at the end to form a loop in the next step).

7 Thread the same length of twine or ribbon through a silk flower (or more than one if you prefer) and then attach the next butterfly as in step 6. Continue in the same way until the garland is the desired length. Tie the ends of the twine or ribbon into hanging loops, to hang the garland on the wall. Glue any buttons in the indentations you made in step 2.

Moth
lights

This project, which can be used for lampshades on either hanging light fixtures or table lamps, was inspired by moths fluttering around a light, which always fascinates children. The materials used for the moths are so light and delicate that their wings flutter gently in the air. Some of the moths are made from paper torn from old books, with the paper's browned edges resembling a moth's wings. I used only subtle neutral tones, but if you prefer you could use brighter colors to make butterflies instead.

materials and equipment

Fusible web

Iron and ironing board

Natural linen fabric

Patterns for three moths
(see page 189)

Dressmaker's shears,
general-purpose scissors,
and small, sharp scissors

Pages from old books,
preferably with brown
edges

Silk organdy

Newspaper and spray
adhesive

Cylindrical lampshades

Sewing needle and
matching thread,
including white or cream

Thick, sharp needle

Silk-flower stamens
(removed from silk
flowers, or bought from
supplier of silk-flower-
making materials)

Small silk flowers and
sequins

Paper silk

Lined paper

Shade with large moths

1 Following the manufacturer's instructions, iron fusible web to the back of the linen and remove the backing paper. Fold the linen in half. Using the pattern for the largest moth and placing the straight edge of the pattern on the fold, cut out one moth from the linen. Using the pattern for the medium moth, cut out a moth from old book paper in the same way. Finally, use the small moth pattern to cut out two moths in the same way from silk organdy.

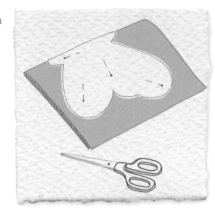

2 Working in a well-ventilated space and covering your work surface with newspaper, spray the backs of the three fabric moths (but not the paper one) with spray adhesive. Position the linen butterfly on the shade, centered between top and bottom, and the other two fabric ones on the shade above and below it, rubbing them gently so they are secure. Sew each in place with a few stitches so they won't fall off over time. Now sew the paper moth in place in the center of the linen moth, with a line of running stitches down the center.

3 Using a thick, sharp needle, make a pattern of holes in the fabric wings (but not the paper ones), puncturing the shade too. If you wish, sew on a pair of antennae to the center moth (see Shade with Moth Cluster, step 2). Finally, sew on silk flowers around the bottom edge of the shade, sewing sequins in the centers. The flowers do not have to be evenly spaced.

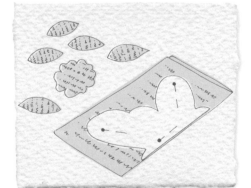

Shade with moth cluster

1 Using the small moth pattern, cut out five moths from paper silk, five from silk organdy, one from old book paper, and three from lined paper (for all of them folding the paper or fabric and positioning the straight edge of the pattern on the fold). Also cut out two simple flower shapes and five leaf shapes from old book paper.

2 To add variety to one or two of the lined-paper moths, make three parallel folds in alternating directions at the center, creating a body. For antennae, attach two silk-flower stamens to the top of each moth body using small stitches—because they are bent, they will stay in place. If you can't find stamens, you can make them with thread, making a few stitches and leaving two 1¼in- (3cm-) long ends, which you knot.

3 Attach the moths to the lampshade by sewing down the center of each with a small running stitch, which will allow the wings to move. Sew on the paper flowers and leaves and some silk flowers (on top of the paper ones and also separately) using small stitches.

Shade with flying moths

1 Fan-pleat the paper silk so it is eight layers thick. Place the straight edge of the small moth pattern on the side with four folds, draw around the shape, and cut out. Open up to reveal four separate moths. Repeat until you have about 20 moths.

2 Thread a needle with white or cream thread, knot the thread, and sew it to the bottom of the shade. Leaving a 6in (15cm) length of thread, stitch the other end to the top of the moth with several stitches, then fasten off the thread. Attach most of the remaining moths in the same way, using varying lengths of thread. Sew a few to the top of the shade in the same way. Add antennae as in Shade with Moth Cluster, step 2.

Balsa wood planes

My father has always made little wooden planes for my children. Created from scraps of wood, corks, bottle tops, and bits and pieces from his toolbox, they are some of my children's favorite possessions. The planes in this project are made from balsa wood, which is easy to saw and does not require a workbench with a vise, so your children can help you make the planes, under close supervision. However, balsa wood is delicate, so the planes are more for decoration than for everyday play. Because they are light, they can easily be hung up or stuck to walls.

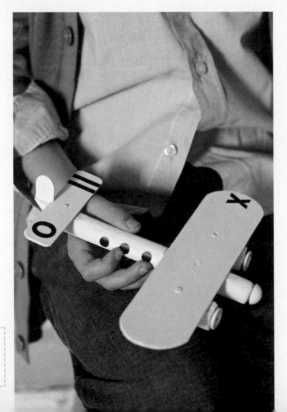

materials and equipment

Balsa wood rod, the thickness of a broom handle

Pencil and metal ruler

Craft knife and cutting mat

Medium-grade sandpaper

Flat balsa wood 2mm thick

Egg cup or small glass

Corks

Awl (bradawl)

Hammer and nails

Wood glue

Wooden ice cream spoons

Latex (emulsion) paints in white and black, and 1in (2.5cm) flat brush

Stickers or dry transfer lettering

Washi tape (a tape made from Japanese washi paper)

White and black buttons, about same diameter as corks

Screw eyes and red ribbons

Plane with black "X" on wing

1 For the airplane fuselage, cut the balsa wood rod to a length of about 8in (20cm) using a craft knife and cutting mat. Hold the sandpaper flat on the work surface and rub one end of the rod against it at a 45-degree angle to make the tail end of the fuselage. Round off any angular edges until it is smooth.

2 With the craft knife, metal ruler, and cutting mat, cut the flat balsa wood into two pieces: one measuring 8¼ x 2in (21 x 5cm) for the wing piece, and the other 4 x 1in (10 x 2.5cm) for the horizontal tail piece. Draw around an egg cup or small glass on each corner of the wing piece, then cut with the craft knife to round off the corners. Repeat for the other three corners of the wing piece. Lightly sand the cut edges. Use sandpaper to round off the corners of the tail piece a little.

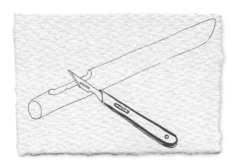

3 With the craft knife, cut a shallow groove out of the top of the fuselage ¾in (2cm) from the nose end. The length of the groove should be just fractionally more than the width of the wing piece. Do not sand the groove. Slot the wing piece into the groove, placing it centrally. Mark where the fuselage comes to on the underside of the wing piece, and then remove the wing piece.

4 For the engines, turn the wing upside down. Slice a sliver off the long side of two corks, and place the flat side of each cork against the wing, with the ends projecting just beyond the wing front. Mark their positions by making a hole through the center of each cork and through the wing using an awl (bradawl). Turn the wing over, with corks in position below and the holes lined up. Wet a nail (to stop the wood splitting) and use a hammer to tap it through the holes in the wing and into the cork. Just before you finish, apply a little glue between each cork and the wing.

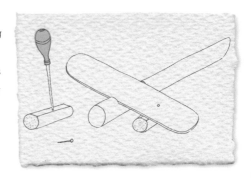

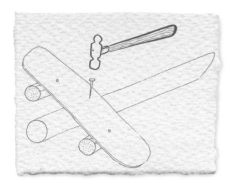

5 Join the fuselage and wing piece at the center using an awl followed by hammering in a wet nail as in step 4, again working from the top and using a little glue at the end of the process to stick the fuselage to the wing.

6 Cut a 2mm-deep x 2mm-wide central slit out of the back edge of the horizontal tail, and also cut a ¾in-(2cm-) deep x 2mm-wide slit into the center of the fuselage at the tail end. For the vertical tail, cut off one end of a wooden ice-cream spoon, cutting it at an angle—it should be 1½in (4cm) long. Slot this vertical tail into the slot in the tail end of the fuselage and also into the slit at the back edge of the horizontal tail, using a little glue. Position the horizontal tail on top of the fuselage. Pin them together using the awl, followed by hammering in a wet nail and adding a little glue, as in step 4.

7 Paint the plane with a coat of white latex (emulsion), allow to dry, and then lightly sand it before applying a second coat. When dry, decorate with stickers, dry transfer lettering, or shapes cut out from washi tape, or let your children paint and decorate the plane. Glue a button to the front of each cork and to the front of the fuselage. (If the buttons have shanks, make a hole first in each cork using an awl/bradawl.)

Other planes

The other planes shown here are variations on the basic method. You can attach screw eyes to the top of the fuselage at front and back, tie ribbons to them, and use these to hang up the plane. Or add a propeller made from two wooden ice cream spoons attached to the nose of the plane as in step 4. (Or attach them to the top of a cork that has nails for feet, as pictured on page 3.)

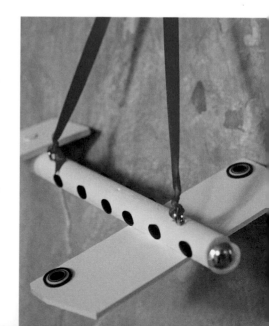

Animal motif
pillows and throw

Some children's drawings are so charming that you want to treasure
them for ever, and this project enables you to capture their best
drawings on pillows and a throw for their bedrooms. Children's
artwork has a beautiful naivety, with simple shapes
that lend themselves well to appliqué and embroidery. The Giraffe
Pillow and Puppy Throw use both techniques, while the Cat Pillow
uses just embroidery—I have explained how to use these three designs
and you can adapt the techniques to your children's own drawings of
their pets or favorite animals. You could also use these techniques
to decorate a readymade pillow cover.

materials and equipment

Simple drawing of an
animal

Pencil and tracing paper
or baking parchment

Dressmaker's shears and
small, sharp scissors

Fine wool in a light
color, for animal motif

Fusible web

Iron and ironing board

Pins

Long ruler

Fabric for pillow or throw

Pillow form

Embroidery needle and
black stranded floss

Sewing machine and
matching thread

Ribbon and small bell
(for Cat Pillow)

Pompom fringe (for
Puppy Throw)

Giraffe pillow

1 Enlarge the drawing to the desired size on a photocopier if necessary, then use a pencil to trace the outline onto tracing paper or baking parchment. (The giraffe's neck had to reach the bottom of the pillow, so I extended it.) Cut a rectangle of light-colored wool large enough for the motif. Following the manufacturer's instructions, iron fusible web to the wrong side, and then pin the tracing paper motif to the right side and cut out the shape. Remove the pins and tracing paper.

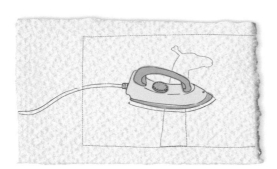

2 Cut one rectangle from the pillow-cover fabric, making it twice the width of the pillow form plus 4in (10cm), and the depth of the pillow form plus 1¼in (3cm). Remove the backing paper from the wool motif. Iron the motif to the right side of the pillow-cover rectangle, centering it between the side edges and aligning the bottom edges.

3 Pin the tracing paper shape to the felt motif again. With an embroidery needle and three strands of floss, embroider running stitch just inside the edge, through both the paper and fabric. At the bottom edge, the running stitch should be ¾in (2cm) from the edge. Use smaller running stitches around the horns and for the mouth. Embroider the ears and the nostril in a very small running stitch. Using six strands of floss, embroider the large spots on the neck and the smaller ones on the head, which are pentagons and hexagons (with five or six straight sides), with a single long stitch for each side. Using six strands, embroider the eye in satin stitch (see Needle Case, step 2, page 100), adding straight stitches for the eyelashes. Very carefully tear away the tracing paper bit by bit, without disturbing the stitching.

4 To make up, turn under, press, and machine stitch a ¼in (5mm) single hem on each of the two side edges. With the cover right side up on the work surface, fold the hemmed sides back on themselves by equal amounts, so they overlap by 3½in (9cm) and the width of the cover is the same as that of the pillow form. The front and back should be right sides together. Pin and stitch ⅝in (1.5cm) seams at the top and bottom edges. Snip off the corners of the seam allowances and turn right side out through the hemmed opening. Insert the pillow form.

Cat pillow

1 Cut one rectangle of pillow-cover fabric, making it twice the width of the pillow form plus 4in (10cm), and the depth of the pillow form plus 1¼in (3cm). Enlarge the drawing to the desired size on a photocopier, then trace the outline onto tracing paper or baking parchment. Pin the paper centrally on the right side of the pillow-cover fabric.

2 With an embroidery needle and three strands of black floss, embroider the design (including the mouth and the circles for the eyes) through the paper and into the fabric, using running stitch. For the eye slits and the triangular nose, use single straight stitches consisting of six strands. For each whisker, use six strands to work a single long stitch. Remove the paper. Turn under the ends of a piece of ribbon and sew this on as a collar. Also sew on a bell. Complete as for the Giraffe Pillow, step 4.

Puppy throw

Cut a piece of fabric to the desired size of the throw. Either stitch pompom trim to all four edges, or fray the side edges (see Floral Wall Hanging, step 1, page 36) and stitch pompom trim to the other two edges. Make the motif as for the Giraffe Pillow, steps 1–3, positioning it near a bottom corner. When embroidering the design use three strands and work running stitch for the outline, and then six strands for the satin stitch eyes, nose, and tail, and for the French knot eye (see Needle Case, step 4, page 100).

TIP

To "frame" the motif, stitch ribbon and/or rickrack to the fabric close to the animal, adding buttons to the corners for extra pizzazz.

Star
light

Children love looking at the stars and learning the names of the constellations, and this starry lampshade will help them to remember their favorites, whether it's the Big Dipper or Gemini. You can find the most familiar constellations in books or on the internet, but choose those that are relatively simple and recognizable. Use sequins for the stars, and off-white embroidery floss to join them together, to look like constellation diagrams. The sequins glint in the light, creating a miniature universe in a child's bedroom.

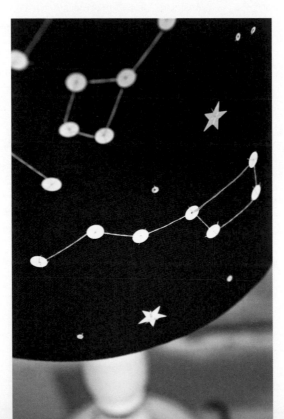

materials and equipment

Constellation diagrams, for reference

Black or dark blue lampshade

Tailor's chalk

Silver or pale-colored sequins: small and medium-size round ones and larger star shapes

Sewing needle and thread to match sequins

Embroidery needle and stranded embroidery floss in off-white

Ribbon or fabric strips, for lamp base

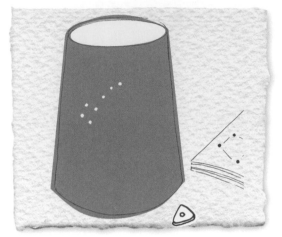

1 Using constellation diagrams for reference, mark the positions of the stars on the lampshade with tailor's chalk. At this point, mark out just one constellation (or two on opposite sides of the shade), rather than all of them, otherwise it can be difficult to see the shapes when the shade has lots of dots on it. There is no need to mark the lines between them.

2 Hand sew each sequin in place, using the star sequins for the larger stars on the constellation diagrams, and the medium-size round ones for the other stars in the constellations.

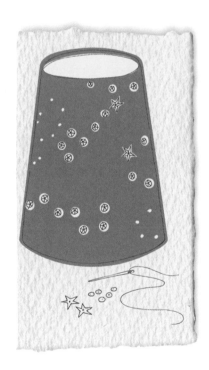

3 Now go back and repeat steps 1 and 2 for the other constellations, again completing one or two before doing the others, and leaving gaps between them.

4 Thread an embroidery needle with three long strands of white floss, and knot the ends together. Starting and finishing on the inside of the shade, embroider lines between the stars, copying the lines in the constellation diagrams and using one long stitch between each pair of stars.

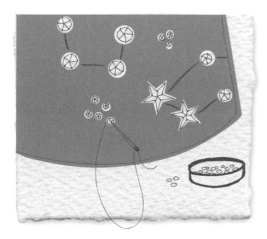

5 Sew little clusters of the small round sequins in gaps between the constellations, to give an all-over pattern.

6 To make the lamp base more interesting, wind lengths of ribbon or fabric strips around it, tucking in the ends to stop it unwinding.

TIP

Be as neat as you can with the stitching on the reverse, as it might show through when the light is turned on. Repeat with the other three strands and then with further lengths.

61

Planet
mobile

This mobile is a stylized representation of our solar system, with the sun at the middle and nine planets (including the dwarf planet Pluto) circling around it. If you want to, you can make the sizes correspond very roughly to the relative size of the planets, choose a color traditionally associated with each planet, and hang the balls in a sequence corresponding to the planets' distance from the sun. However, the land/sea detail on the earth, the moon orbiting the earth, and Saturn's rings give enough detail to suggest our solar system without your having to worry about being technically accurate. This mobile is for fun and inspiration.

materials and equipment

11 polystyrene balls in various sizes from ¾in (2cm) to 3in (7.5cm)

Thick cardboard

Compass, pencil, and tape measure

Cutting mat and scalpel or craft knife

White glue

Flat paintbrush 1in (2.5cm) wide

Acrylic paints in various colors including bright yellow, soft yellow, red, a sludgy turquoise, gray, and green

Eggcup or small dish

12in (30cm) embroidery hoop (inner ring only)

World map or globe, for reference

Small piece of stiff wire, such as florist's stub wire

Small, sharp scissors

Nylon fishing line

Very long needle (available from craft stores)

Skewer (optional)

Hook (to go in ceiling)

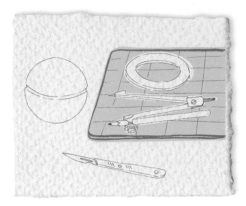

1 Decide which ball will be for which planet, the sun, and the moon, using the largest ball for the sun, then balls in descending sizes for Jupiter, Saturn, Uranus and Neptune, Earth, Venus, Mars, Mercury, the moon, and the dwarf planet Pluto. For Saturn's ring, on thick cardboard draw a circle that is slightly smaller than the diameter of the ball that will be Saturn, using a compass and pencil. (It can be difficult to measure the diameter of a ball, but you can calculate it by simply measuring the circumference and dividing this by 3.14.) Draw another circle around it, ⅜in (1cm) away from the first. Place the cardboard on a cutting mat and cut out the two circles with a scalpel. Now cut the ball in half through the center. Place the ring between the two halves, smoothing any rough edges with your finger, and glue together. Leave the glue to dry.

2 With the flat brush, paint the balls in different colors of acrylic paints, using bright yellow for the sun, soft yellow for Saturn, red for Mars, sludgy turquoise for earth, gray for the moon, and colors of your own choice for the others. It's easiest to place a ball in an eggcup or small dish and paint as much as you

can, then when it is dry turn it over and paint the rest. For Saturn, paint the ring at the same time as the ball and in the same color. Paint the inner ring of the embroidery hoop gray.

3 When the turquoise paint on the earth is dry, paint the continents in green, using a world map or globe for reference. It doesn't have to be exact—just an impression of land will be enough. When dry, pin the moon to the earth with a length of wire, twisting one end to prevent it from sliding through.

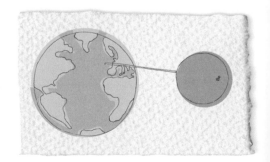

4 Tie a length of fishing line to the embroidery hoop, leaving a very long end. Stretch the line across the center and tie the other end to the opposite side of the hoop, again leaving a very long end. Repeat for three more lengths of fishing line, spacing them equally so the hoop is divided into eight equal segments, like spokes of a wheel.

5 Cut ten lengths of fishing line about 15in (38cm) long. For the smaller planets, thread one of these through a needle that is longer than the diameter of the ball. Knot one end several times. Push the needle straight through the polystyrene and pull it out the other side until

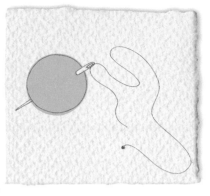

the knot stops it, then push the knot inside the polystyrene to hide it. For the larger planets, you may need to make a hole and then slide the fishing line through, or make a hole at each side with a long needle and then push the needle through, threaded end first. Or you could use a skewer to make the hole and then slide the fishing line through.

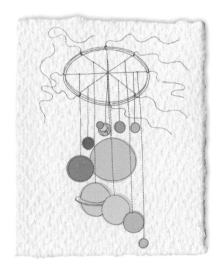

6 Sit on a chair and place the hoop between your knees. Tie the sun's fishing line to the center of the fishing line "spokes," so that it is hanging about 6in (15cm) below the hoop. Work your way around the hoop, tying one planet to each "spoke" so that each is the same distance from

the hoop but hangs a little lower than the previous (adjacent) one, until the final one hangs about 12in (30cm) from the hoop. Attach them in the order of the planets' distance from the sun, starting with Mercury (the closest), then Venus, Earth, Mars, Jupiter, Saturn, Uranus, Neptune and Pluto. Pluto will hang from the same "spoke" as Mercury, but farther away from the sun.

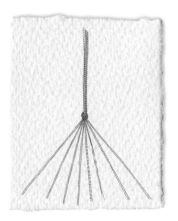

7 To make the mobile hang straight, adjust the positions of the planets if you wish by sliding their pieces of fishing line along the "spokes." Pull up the eight loose ends of fishing line and tie them securely together to create a single hanging point. Snip off any excess fishing line, and hang the mobile from a hook in the ceiling.

When walking around flea markets, I am always drawn to piles of paper collectibles, especially old trading cards, such as baseball cards, tea cards, cigarette cards, and even bubblegum cards. Vintage trading cards are easy to find and often sold cheaply in bundles with rubber bands around them. The set shown here is of old racing cars but you can also find birds, butterflies, flowers, animals, sportsmen, and aircraft, as well as vintage children's card games. Instead of relegating the cards to a box in a drawer, here's a good way of showing them off and also providing colorful decorations for a child's room. However, make sure that none of the cards are valuable!

QUICK IDEAS
Vintage card garland

* You can leave the caption on the back of the card visible, or glue two cards back to back. Another approach is to cut out colored paperboard the same size as the card and glue it to the back. If you have duplicates of any cards, you could cut out the illustration from one of them and stick it on top of the paperboard.

* Thread your sewing machine with different colors for the top and bobbin threads, and set the stitch length to a long stitch. Run the machine without anything under the needle while pulling the thread, to create a "string" consisting of the two threads twisted together. Stitch across each card but stitch without anything under the needle for about ⅜in (1cm) after each card to create small gaps between the cards. When the garland is the desired length, stitch again without anything under the needle to create extra "string" at the other end. Use the "string" at the beginning and end of the garland to hang it from hooks or picture hangers on the wall.

Height board

Many adults remember having their height measured and marked on a door frame or wall when they were children, but this project allows you to take the record with you if you move house, providing a wonderful display object with real family history. Each child can have their own board, a stripy reminder of their growth, like the rings inside a tree, because the bands of color build up as the child grows.

✳ Buy a planed plank of wood—the one shown here was 78in (2m) long, 6in (15cm) wide, and ¾in (2cm) thick. If you choose pine, seal the knots with knotting compound, to prevent oily stains from seeping through over time. Paint the board with undercoat and then white eggshell paint, allowing it to dry after each coat. Use transfer lettering or a stencil to add the child's name and date of birth at the top.

✳ Use a long ruler, set square, and pencil to mark measurements at intervals along the left-hand edge of the board. Mark every 6–12in if you prefer inches and feet, or 20–25cm if you prefer metric. The "0" mark should be at the bottom of the board because it will sit on the floor. Use transfer lettering, number stickers, and/or stencils in a variety of styles to add numbers and lines at these markings.

✳ Mark the child's height with a pencil and paint a colored band below the mark using acrylic paints or tester pots of latex (emulsion) paint, taking care not to cover up any numbers. To ensure the edges of the band are crisp, stick masking tape just outside the edges before painting, then gently remove the tape after the paint has dried. If paint has leaked under the tape, use a scalpel to scratch it away.

✳ When the paint is dry, use transfer lettering, stickers and/or stencils to record the child's age on the right-hand edge at the appropriate height mark, using a variety of styles to add a graphic quality. You could also add the exact height on the left-hand edge opposite the child's age, and write the date on the the chart so that you have an exact record.

✳ To hang the board on the wall, drill a hole at the top, thread strong string through, and loop this over a hook in the wall.

Birdcage with string lights

Coiling string lights in the base of an old birdcage that you have decorated is a simple way to create a delightful bedside light. At night the string lights glow as your child drifts off to sleep, and in daylight the glass beads shimmer. Strips of patterned fabric add a romantic softness and can tie in with the color scheme or echo the fabrics used elsewhere in the room.

✷ First paint the birdcage—I used a tester pot of latex (emulsion) in a sludgy gray-green but white would work, too. Leave to dry.

✷ Cut scraps of silk ribbon and patterned fabric into strips. Tie them to the bars with knots, hanging them high enough that they won't rest on the bulbs. Sew or tie glass beads and semiprecious stones to the bottoms of the ribbons, varying the heights.

✷ If the electric plug is too large to fit between the bars, feed the string lights through the bars from the outside little by little, with the plug remaining outside the cage so it can be plugged in. Coil the lights into a nest in the base of the birdcage.

CHAPTER 3 # Play

With a little spark to invigorate their imaginations, children will play happily for hours, and the projects in this chapter will give them precisely that. They range from dressing-up costumes to sailboats, from vintage-style dolls to matchbox mice, and from unusual blackboards to a wishing board. All are so charming that even if they are not tidied up after play, they will still make you smile.

Play
sail

This simple "sailboat" with flag will transport your young pirate or explorer to faraway places. The sail can be personalized with the child's name or age, and the large pocket is perfect for maps, toys, and, of course, edible supplies for the long voyage. I used an old tin bath as a boat but a cardboard box would do just as well. Simply remove a picture or mirror from the wall and hang the sail from the screw, then tie the bottom ropes to furniture, ready to sail away on imaginary adventures.

materials and equipment

Dressmaker's shears and small, sharp scissors

Canvas

Set square (or large book or magazine)

Long ruler and tape measure

Pencil or tailor's chalk

Iron and ironing board

Pins

Sewing machine

Matching sewing thread

Striped ribbon

Kit for 10 jumbo grommets, with holes of about ½in (12mm) across

Fusible web

Denim

Patterns for star and for skull and crossbones (see page 188)

¼in- (5mm-) wide rope (or strong ribbon or string)

Stick 24in (60cm) long, for pirate flag

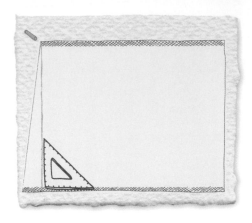

Sail with pocket

1 Using dressmaker's shears, cut out a 67 x 55in (170 x 140cm) rectangle of canvas. Lay the canvas on your work surface and check that the cut edge is straight, using a set square (or the corner of a large book or magazine). If necessary, use the set square (or book or magazine) and a long ruler to draw a new cutting line at right angles to the selvedge, and cut along this line with the dressmaker's shears.

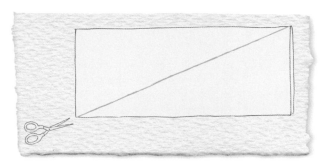

2 Fold the fabric in half lengthwise. With a pencil or tailor's chalk, draw a diagonal line from the top corner at the fold to the bottom corner that isn't on the fold. With the dressmaker's shears, cut along this line through both layers, and then open out the triangle.

3 Turn under a ⅝in (1.5cm) hem on all three edges, press, pin in place, and stitch. Pin two lengths of ribbon to the sail, parallel to the bottom edge, dividing the triangle into three sections; you can either leave long ends hanging down, as I've done, or turn under ¼in (5mm) at each end. Stitch the ribbons in place.

4 For the pocket, cut out a 15 x 12in (38 x 30cm) rectangle from canvas. Turn under and press a ⅝in (1.5cm) hem on the side edges and fray the top and bottom edge by teasing out threads parallel to the edge (see Floral Wall Hanging, step 1, page 36). Following the manufacturer's instructions, apply three grommets along the top edge of the pocket, and one grommet to each corner of the sail. Pin the pocket at the center of the bottom portion of the sail, and topstitch in place along the side and bottom edges.

PLAY

7 6

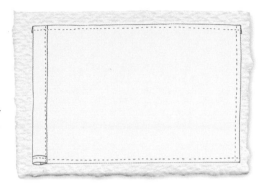

Pirate flag

1 Cut out a 20 x 14in (50 x 35cm) rectangle from the canvas left over from cutting out the triangle for the sail. Turn ⅝in (1.5cm) to the wrong side along the long bottom edge; press, pin, and stitch.

Now turn ¼in (5mm) and then a further ⅝in (1.5cm) to the right side along one short side edge; press, pin, and machine stitch. Finally, turn ⅝in (1.5cm) to the wrong side along the other short side edge and the long top edge; press, pin, and stitch. Doing the hems in this sequence produces a channel at one side, with an opening at the bottom but not at the top.

5 Following the manufacturer's instructions, iron fusible web to the wrong side of a piece of denim. Using the star pattern, draw a star on the backing paper. Also draw the mirror image of each initial or number. Cut out the shapes, remove the backing paper, and iron them in place on the sail. Tie a length of rope to the grommet at each of the two bottom corners of the sail, and tie the other end of each length to a piece of furniture. Hang the top grommet from a very secure screw in the wall, or use a third length of rope to tie it to a tree.

2 Using the pattern, cut out a skull and two crossbones from the denim that you backed with fusible web in step 5. Following the manufacturer's instructions, remove the backing paper and iron the motifs to the right side of the canvas. If desired, cut out another skull and crossbones and iron them to the wrong side of the canvas as decoration. Apply a grommet to each of the four corners. Insert the stick into the channel.

TIP

You could hang the sail outdoors, too. Attach a rope to the top grommet and tie the other end to a tree branch, then tie the bottom ropes to tent pegs in the ground, or simply wind them securely around heavy rocks. The wind will fill the sail as though it were a real boat.

Vintage-style
dolls

Recreate the old-fashioned charm of antique china dolls, and make something precious to look after and keep. It's fun to watch the dolls' personalities develop as you paint their faces on. You could loosely base a doll on someone you know, or on the child you are making it for, personalizing the doll with the child's eye color and hair color and perhaps with fabric to match their bedroom. Because they are made from clay, the dolls are quite delicate and so are most suitable for older children who will play with them carefully, or for display on a shelf out of reach of younger children. They also make delightful Christmas tree ornaments (hung safely on the higher branches).

materials and equipment

Air-drying clay in white

Ruler and craft knife

Chopping board

Wooden skewers

Fine sandpaper or emery board

Reusable adhesive putty and coffee mug

Acrylic paints and fine artist's brush

Pins and small, sharp scissors

Patterns for doll's body and wings (see page 189)

Fabric scraps

Sewing needle and matching thread

Batting (wadding)

Strong glue

Fine wire and tiny beads (for tiara, crown, or halo)

Strong scissors

Cotton organza or other stiff or starched fabric

Narrow ribbon or lace

Tiny buttons, sequins, and silk flowers

1 For each doll, roll some clay into two sausages, ⅜in (8mm) in diameter: one of them 8½in (22cm) long for the legs, and the other 6¼in (16cm) long for the arms. Bend these in half and cut with a craft knife, to form two legs and two arms. Roll out a ¾in (2cm) ball for the head. Make a few sets at a time, so you'll have more than one doll and also will have spares in case any get broken. Place them on a chopping board and use a skewer to make a hole through the center of each head, and through the top of each arm and leg. Gently squeeze the other end of each arm flat to create a hand. Leave to dry on the chopping board at least overnight or until they are totally dry.

2 Lightly sand the arms, legs, and heads with fine sandpaper or an emery board to remove any rough edges. Place some reusable adhesive putty on an upturned mug and stick each head on it while you paint the face and hair using acrylic paints and a fine artist's brush. Also paint shoes on one end of each leg (and, if you wish, red fingernails on the hands).

3 For each doll, pin the pattern for the body to a folded fabric scrap, and cut out two pieces. Pin one piece to the other with right sides together. Using running stitch or backstitch (see Butterfly Table Lamp, step 2, page 24), sew ¼in (5mm) seams down the side edges, leaving the top and bottom edges open. Turn right side out and stuff the body with batting (wadding) through the opening at the bottom edge.

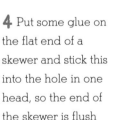

4 Put some glue on the flat end of a skewer and stick this into the hole in one head, so the end of the skewer is flush with the top of the head. Leave to dry. Repeat for the other dolls. For a doll with a tiara, crown, or halo, push a length of fine wire through with the skewer and pull enough wire through at the top to make a ring (which will be completed in step 8).

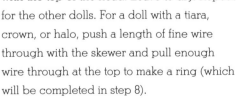

5 With strong scissors, cut the skewer about 1½in (4cm) below the bottom of the head. Wind any excess wire around the skewer. Poke the skewer into the padded body so that the top of the fabric neck meets the bottom of the head. Carefully glue the inside of the fabric neck to the skewer; leave to dry. With a needle and a knotted double length of thread, make a stitch in the fabric and then wind the thread tightly around the neck enough times to create a firm neck; secure with a knot.

6 Sew the opening at the bottom edge of the body closed. Sew each limb to the body through the hole at the top of the limb, and then wind the thread around the stitches to neaten the attachments.

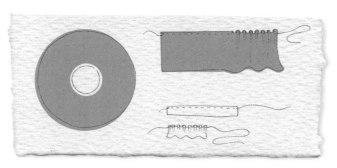

7 For a skirt, make a circle pattern with a radius (distance from center to edge) equal to the desired length of the skirt, and use this to cut a circle of organza or other stiff fabric. Cut a hole in the center to fit over the body. Or for a different style of skirt, cut a rectangle of fabric, sew running stitch along the top edge, leaving long ends, and pull the thread (while holding the other end) to gather it up around the waist; knot the thread ends. You can use this same technique on two smaller rectangles to make ruffled sleeves to fit over the top of the arms. Wrap narrow ribbon around the waist, sewing the ends together at the back, to create a cummerbund, or use a wider piece of lace as a bodice. Experiment to devise your own variations.

8 Sew on buttons, sequins, flowers, and ribbons to finish. For an angel or fairy, pin the wings pattern to a folded piece of organza, with the straight edge on the fold, and cut out. Open out and attach to the back of the doll by sewing running stitch down the center. To make a tiara, crown, or halo, thread beads onto the wire sticking out of the head (see step 4), and twist the end of the wire around itself to fasten. If you wish, tie a narrow ribbon around the wire beneath the tiara or crown, which can be used to hang the angel or fairy from the Christmas tree.

Busy bumblebee
costume

This costume was the result of a washing accident, when a sweater of my husband's was put in too hot a wash. I decided to turn a disaster into something positive by shrinking it further until it would fit a child, and because the fuzzy texture of the shrunken, felted sweater reminded me of a bumblebee, it became a bumblebee costume! I love the stiffness of felted wool, which makes stitching the ribbon stripes on without puckering much easier than with a stretchy fabric. The detachable wings can be as simple or complicated as you like. Teamed with black leggings and a spray-painted pair of old Deely Bobbers, it makes a perfect outfit for a young child to wear while buzzing busily about the house or at a birthday party.

materials and equipment

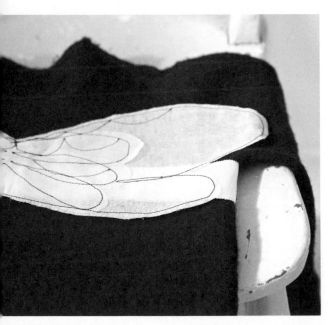

Black sweater, too large in size

Yellow grosgrain ribbon and/or velvet ribbon, about 1–1½ in (2.5–4cm) wide

Small, sharp scissors and dressmaker's shears

Pins

Sewing needle and yellow thread

Yellow grosgrain ribbon ¼in (5mm) wide

Organdy or other stiff fabric, for wings

Patterns for bee's outer wings and inner wings (see page 185)

Sewing machine with embroidery foot

1¼ in (3cm) square of sew-on hook-and-loop tape such as Sew-On Velcro, in black

Pair of Deely Bobbers (antennae on a hair band)

Black spray paint and old newspaper

Black leggings or tights, to wear with top

1 Wash the sweater in a hot cycle until it is the correct size and is felted. The one pictured here started as a man's sweater, 50 percent wool and 50 percent acrylic. After the first (accidental) shrink it was a couple of sizes smaller; after the second (deliberate) shrink, at 140°F (60°C), it was still not small enough; and after the third, at 200°F (95°C), it was just right. It is always difficult to judge how materials will shrink, so try it little by little. The sleeves can always be rolled up or cut and hemmed if necessary.

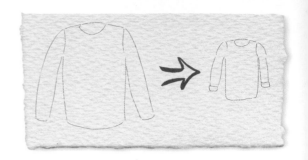

2 For each stripe, cut a length of ribbon 1–1½in (2.5–4cm) wide and long enough to go all the way around the body of the sweater, plus 1in (2.5cm). Pin the first one about ½in (1cm) from the bottom edge of the sweater, starting at one side seam and turning under the end by ¼in (5mm). When you have pinned it and are back to the starting point, cut off any excess ribbon and turn under ¼in (5mm) so the two turned-under ends butt together. With a sewing needle and yellow thread, sew the top edge and the bottom edge to the sweater with tiny, unnoticeable stitches. Also sew the two turned-under ends together.

3 In the same way, pin and sew on another length of ribbon around the chest and back just beneath the sleeves. Sew on a third in between the other two—it will look more interesting if they aren't equidistant.

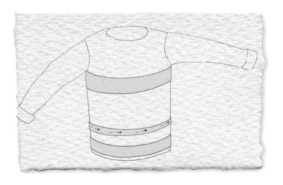

4 Now cut a length of narrow yellow ribbon to go around the front neck edge only, between the shoulder seams, adding ½in (1cm) extra. (Not putting the ribbon on the back neck edge will allow the sweater to stretch enough to pull it on over the head.) Turn under ¼in (5mm) at each end and sew it to the sweater along the top and bottom edges and the ends.

5 Fold the organdy in half. Place the pattern for the outer wings on the fold, pin in place, and cut out the outer-wings piece from the organdy. Repeat to cut out another outer wings piece. Also cut out six inner wings from the organdy.

6 Fit the embroidery foot on the sewing machine and set the machine to freestitch. Place one outer-wings piece on top of the other, with the edges even, and join them together around the edges using machine embroidery. Pin the six inner wings on top, three each side, with the pointed ends toward the center. Machine embroider these in place too, adding extra stitching if you wish.

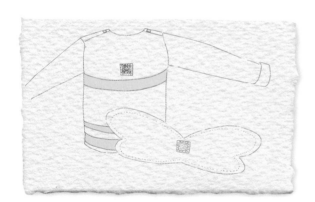

7 Fit the regular presser foot to the machine. Pin and machine stitch the soft, looped side of a 1¼in (3cm) square of black sew-on hook-and-loop tape to the center back of the sweater on the right side. (That way it won't stick to itself when the wings are removed and the sweater is washed.) Pin and machine stitch the hooked side at top center of the wings on the underside.

8 Working outdoors or in a well-ventilated room, spray paint the Deely Bobbers black, and leave to dry on old newspaper. Team them and the striped sweater with black leggings or tights to complete your little bumblebee outfit.

Fairy
costume

With this costume, what little girl wouldn't want to become a fairy—even a messy, cookie-loving little fairy with chocolate around her mouth? This delightful costume is perfect for special occasions such as a dressing-up party, or even for a flower girl to wear at a wedding, but it will undoubtedly also prove irresistible at home. The wraparound skirt can grow with your fairy. As it is translucent, stripy leggings, pink tights, or big pants will look sweet underneath.

materials and equipment

Silk organdy in pink for wings, skirt, and tiara and in a different color for petals on skirt

Pins

Patterns for wings, petal, and flower (see page 187)

Dressmaker's shears and small, sharp scissors

Sewing machine

Sewing needle and matching thread

Four large handfuls of sequins

39in (1m) of lace ribbon

Brooch

2½ yd (2.3m) of pink ribbon 1½ in (4cm) wide

Rhinestones for skirt waistband and tiara

Inexpensive tiara (preferably not plastic)

Silk leaf, two feathers, and scrap of lace ribbon

Stripy leggings, tights, or big pants, plus pink tank top and ballet slippers, to wear with skirt and wings

Fairy wings

1 For the wings you need a piece of organdy at least 33 x 17in (84 x 44cm). Fold it in half lengthwise and then in half crosswise. Pin the wing pattern so the straight edge is on the second fold in the fabric. Cut around the outside using dressmaker's shears, cutting through all four layers. Open out the two resulting identical B-shapes.

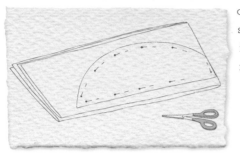

2 Pin the two wing pieces with wrong sides together and machine stitch a ⅝in (1.5cm) seam around the edges, leaving a small opening in the seam at one end. Leave the seam allowance on the outside to form a decorative feature. You can trim it if you wish, but don't trim too close to the stitching. Pour two handfuls of sequins through the opening, then stitch the opening closed.

3 Cut the lace ribbon in two, fold each piece in half, and sew to the outer corners of the wings. These ribbons will be tied around the child's wrists to hold the wings in place. Iron the fabric, avoiding the sequins, then shake the wings to distribute the sequins evenly. Pin a brooch to the center of the wings—this will be fastened to the tank top to secure the wings at the center.

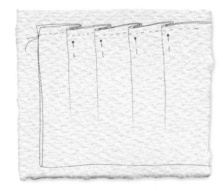

Fairy skirt

1 Cut a 53 x 29in (133 x 73cm) piece of organdy, and fold it in half lengthwise. The fold will be at the lower edge of the skirt. Baste the two long edges together. Fold and pin the fabric into pleats about 2in (5cm) apart along this basted edge until the pleated top edge measures about 38in (96cm); baste.

2 Use the petal pattern to cut out seven petals from contrasting organdy. Position these along the pleated edge, overlapping the lower part of the petals a little. Pin in place. Baste, remove all pins, and then stitch a ⅝in (1.5cm) seam along the entire edge.

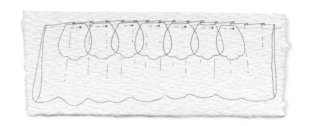

3 On each side edge, turn over both layers together to form a ⅝in (1.5cm) hem and pin. Stitch the hems in place, leaving the top 2in (5cm) unstitched on one of the hems. Pour two large handfuls of sequins into the skirt through the opening, and then stitch the opening closed.

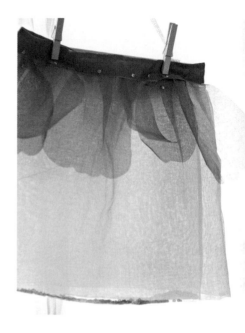

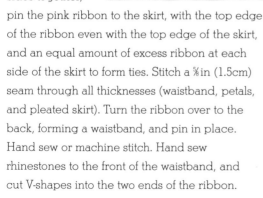

4 With right sides together, pin the pink ribbon to the skirt, with the top edge of the ribbon even with the top edge of the skirt, and an equal amount of excess ribbon at each side of the skirt to form ties. Stitch a ⅝in (1.5cm) seam through all thicknesses (waistband, petals, and pleated skirt). Turn the ribbon over to the back, forming a waistband, and pin in place. Hand sew or machine stitch. Hand sew rhinestones to the front of the waistband, and cut V-shapes into the two ends of the ribbon.

Tiara

Pleat or fold the pink organdy into four layers and, using the flower pattern, cut out lots of flower shapes from it, cutting out four at a time. Sew four flowers together with a rhinestone at the center, and attach the flowers to the tiara by sewing at the back, where the stitches will be hidden. Fold some of the flowers into quarters to create a bud shape, using just two flowers for each of these rather than four. Continue making and sewing on flowers and buds until the tiara looks full but is not completely covered. Sew a silk leaf and feathers to the tiara, and tie on a length of lace ribbon so the ends hang down.

Spotty dotty chairs

Here is a quick and easy way to revamp an old set of children's chairs—just give them a lick of paint and add a simple graphic motif, and they will brighten up any children's party. I limited myself to three colors, with each used for the background on one of the chairs and the other two colors used for spots and dots of varying size. If you have a matching table, you could treat it in the same way. In fact, you could even stick matching spots on the walls!

materials and equipment

Set of old children's chairs

Water, sponge, and sugar soap

Old newspaper

Undercoat

Flat paintbrushes, 1½in (4cm) and ½in (1.5cm) wide

Water- or oil-based eggshell paint in assorted colors (one per chair)

Masking tape

Scissors (optional)

Craft knife and cutting mat

Frisket masking film in matte finish (see Tip)

Compass and pencil

Small brush (optional)

1 Wash the chairs with water, a sponge, and sugar soap, and leave to dry on some old newspaper. When dry, paint the chairs all over with undercoat using a 1½in (4cm) flat brush. Leave to dry, and then paint the first chair's seat and back with one color. (If you want the legs and back supports to be the same color as the seat and back, you can paint them now, too.) Apply two or three coats, leaving the paint to dry after each coat. Repeat for the other two chairs, using the other paint colors.

2 If you want the legs and back supports to be different in color from the back and seat, paint them with your chosen color. If you want to use more than one color on the legs, you need to mask along the horizontal line where the two colors will meet, such as above the feet, or partway up the legs. Stick masking tape just above this line and then apply the first color below the tape, painting right up to it. When dry, apply one or two more coats, allowing it to dry after each coat.

3 If using more than one color on the legs, carefully remove and discard the tape, and put some more tape along the edge of the painted area (over the painted portion). Apply two or three coats of the new color above the tape, allowing it to dry after each coat. Remove the masking tape.

4 With scissors or a craft knife and cutting mat, cut out a square of Frisket masking film that is larger than the size of the desired circle. Use a compass and pencil to draw a circle of the desired size in the center of the square. Place the square on a cutting mat and cut along the outline of the circle with a craft knife. Remove the circle, leaving a circle stencil. Repeat for every spot on each chair.

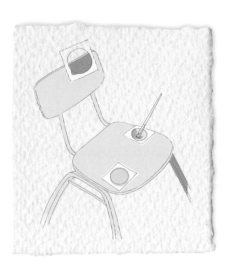

5 Place the stencils (which are self-adhesive) in position, and smooth down with your fingers. Some can be positioned as semicircles at the edges. With a ½in (1.5cm) brush and a different paint color than the chair, apply the paint within the window in the stencil, painting away from the edges. Repeat for the other spots. Allow to dry, and then apply a second coat to each spot. When dry or nearly dry, remove each stencil carefully.

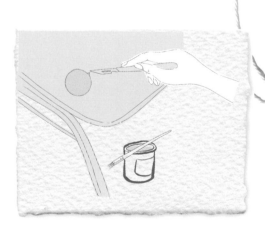

6 If there has been any seepage of paint under the edges, touch up with a small brush and the appropriate paint color, or gently scrape the drip away with the craft knife.

TIP

Frisket masking film is plastic sheet or specially treated paper with adhesive backing which can be used to mask part of an image while painting. You can draw on the paper or on the matte film and then cut it to shape, so it allows you to mask curves, which is difficult to do with masking tape. It is ideal for making stencils.

Matchbox
mice

The inspiration for these mice came from a vintage curio shop, whose owner introduced my family and me to a little wild mouse who lived in a teacup on a shelf. His little nose would emerge as he sniffed the air and nibbled a cookie, and we were captivated. The felt mice in this project could have this fabric-covered matchbox as a more sumptuous mouse-house, with perhaps a teacup as a vacation home! Children will love playing with the mice, and you could even create bedding and pillows for them. Make them as gifts for friends' children or for your own—or use hand sewing rather than a sewing machine and then involve your children in making them.

materials and equipment

Pattern for mouse (see page 188)

Felt in white, gray, or black

Two fine cotton print fabrics

Small, sharp scissors

Pins

10½in (27cm) length of ribbon or leather string, for tail

Sewing machine

Sewing thread in black and white

Batting (wadding)

Sewing needle

Embroidery needle and pink floss

Two black sequins

Latex (emulsion) paint in white and ½in (1.5cm) flat brush

Large matchbox

Acrylic paint in chosen color

Tape measure and ruler

Double-sided tape

Tailor's chalk

Mouse

1 Using the pattern, cut out two mouse pieces and two ears from white, gray, or black felt, and cut out two inner ears from a print fabric. Pin the two mouse pieces together, sandwiching ½in (1.5cm) of the ribbon or leather string between the layers as a tail.

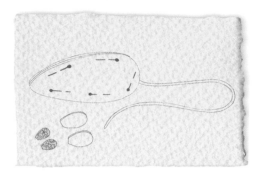

2 Machine stitch a ⅛in (3mm) seam around the edge, using matching thread and leaving a ¾in (2cm) opening at the center of the bottom edge. Stuff the mouse with batting (wadding), and then stitch the opening closed.

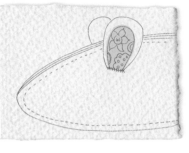

3 Place a print inner ear on top of one felt ear. Use a sewing needle and matching thread to hand sew them simultaneously to one side of the top of the head, making the stitches only at the bottom (so the ears can move) but ensuring the pieces are securely attached. Repeat to attach the other ear and inner ear to the other side of the top of the head.

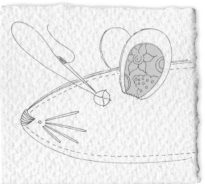

4 With an embroidery needle and pink floss, embroider a small nose in satin stitch. In black thread (for white or gray felt) or pink floss (for black felt), sew four long stitches in a fan shape on each side of the nose as whiskers; the knot will show, so it can be part of the effect. Sew on sequins for the eyes using matching thread.

Matchbox

1 Using a flat brush, paint the outside of the matchbox case with white latex (emulsion) paint so that the lettering won't show through the fine cotton fabric. Paint the inside and outside of the inner box with the acrylic color. Leave till the paint is dry.

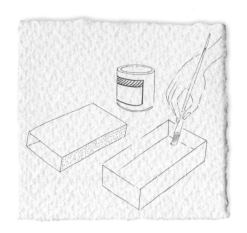

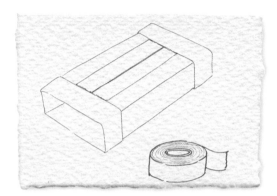

2 Measure and cut out a rectangle from one of the fabrics—it should be as wide as the length of the matchbox case, and as long as the circumference plus ½in (1.5cm) for an overlap. Stick double-sided tape all around the case at both ends, and stick two strips side by side down the middle of the back.

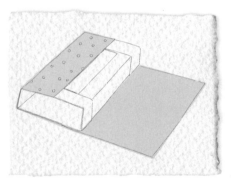

3 Remove the backing from the tape and start sticking the fabric to the case at the middle of the back, covering one of the strips of tape running down the center. Wrap the fabric around the case, with the edges aligned. When you get back to the beginning, stick the end of the fabric to the other strip of tape, trimming off any excess fabric.

4 With tailor's chalk, draw around the inner box on the other fabric. Cut out the rectangle and stick it to the base of the inner box on the inside using double-sided tape. Slide the inner box inside the case, and put the mouse inside.

Needle case
and sewing box

A needle case like a small fabric book is one of the first things I made at school, when I was six or seven, and my mother has kept it in her sewing box all these years. Based on my original needle case, this project is designed to foster an enjoyment of sewing from a young age. It includes a sewing box in which to keep the needle case along with the child's other sewing tools and materials. Imagine a box overflowing with beautiful ribbons, embroidery floss and threads, buttons, and scraps of fabric—the child will want to pick up a needle and thread there and then! They could perhaps even help to make the needle case, learning how to sew the simple embroidery stitches that decorate it.

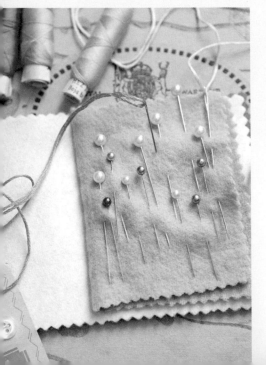

materials and equipment

Tailor's chalk and ruler

Set square (or large book or magazine)

Scraps of felt in three colors (I used gray, cream, and pink)

Pinking shears and small, sharp scissors

Embroidery needle and stranded floss in light green, lime, cream, orange, pink, and lilac (or colors of your choice)

3/8in (1cm) button

6in (15cm) piece of narrow ribbon to match a floss color

Wooden box or shoebox, white paint, and flat brush, for sewing box

Brown paper and patterned cellophane tape or Japanese washi tape (a tape made from Japanese washi paper)—optional

Needle case

1 Using tailor's chalk, a ruler, and a set square if you have one, measure and mark out a 6¼ x 4in (16 x 10cm) rectangle on one piece of felt, for the cover of the "book." If you aren't using a set square, use the corner of a magazine, book, or table to make sure the corners are square. Cut out with pinking shears. In the same way, mark and cut out a 6 x 3¾in (15 x 9.5cm) rectangle from each of the other two colors of felt.

2 Fold the larger piece in half crosswise and crease the fold. Use tailor's chalk to draw the right-hand flower stem ⅝in (1.5cm) from the right-hand edge of this rectangle, stopping about 1¼in (3cm) from the top edge. With an embroidery needle and three strands of light green floss, embroider this stem in running stitch. Near the bottom of the stem, draw a small leaf in tailor's chalk and embroider it using satin stitch (straight stitches side by side within an outline), as shown here.

3 Embroider the other five stems in the same way, with the left-hand stem ⅜in (1cm) from the central crease, and stopping the stitching between ⅝in (1.5cm) and 2½in (6.5cm) from the top, so the stems are all different lengths. Embroider leaves on some of them, and use lime instead of light green for some of the stems and leaves. To add variety, you could use detached chain stitch (see step 6) for some leaves, and backstitch (see Butterfly Table Lamp, step 2, page 24) instead of running stitch for some stems.

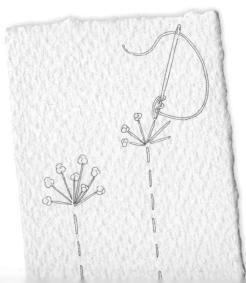

4 For the flower head on the left and the one in the center, use two strands of cream floss to embroider straight stitches of uneven length, all starting at the top of the stem and radiating outward and upward. Now, using six strands of orange for one flower and of pink for the other, add a French knot at the top of each cream straight stitch. To work a French knot, bring the needle out at this point, and hold the thread taut with your other hand as you twist the needle around the floss twice. Now insert the needle back into the fabric, pulling the twist down the needle.

5 Make the pink flower head (second from left) using straight stitches all starting at the top of the stem and fanning outward and upward, with the longest stitches at the center and shortest at the sides to create an even curve. For the cream flower head on the far right, use six strands in a version of eyelet stitch, with all the straight stitches radiating out from the same central hole to create a roughly circular shape as shown here. Add a pink French knot at the center (see step 4).

6 Use detached chain stitch (also known as lazy daisy stitch) for the small cream flower and the lilac flower. Using six strands, bring the needle up at the center and insert it at the same hole, leaving a loop. Bring it up again at the outer end of the loop, on top of the floss, and insert it just on the other side of the floss, making a tiny stitch to hold the loop. Repeat around the center so that the loops form daisy petals. Finally, add an orange French knot at the center (see step 4).

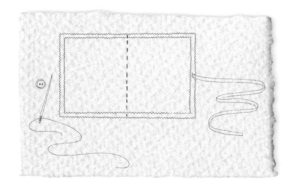

7 Place the embroidered felt rectangle on top of the other two. Sew the three layers together down the creased center with running stitch using six strands of pink floss. Using contrasting floss, sew a button to the top layer in the center of the right-hand edge. Sew a 6in (15cm) length of narrow ribbon to the underside of the top layer in the center of the left-hand edge. When the "book" is closed, you can wind this around the button to keep it closed. Use the "pages" to hold needles and pins.

Sewing box

Paint a wooden box or shoebox white (or use a beautiful large tin or a shoebox decorated as for the Matchbox, page 97), and fill it with sewing treasures such as ribbons, buttons, thread, and floss. I removed the labels from skeins of floss and replaced them with brown paper wrapped around the skeins, held together with patterned tape.

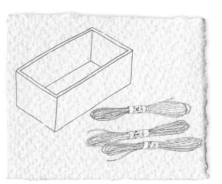

QUICK IDEAS
Artist's
palette blackboards

Youngsters find blackboards irresistible for playing quick games of tic-tac-toe, leaving messages, or drawing pictures, and you can cunningly slip in the occasional spelling practice or multiplication table. These blackboards are easy to make from artist's palettes and blackboard paint, and are handy because they are hung from the thumb hole and so are easy to take down and write on or erase. Their organic shapes are so attractive that I hang them in a group as an ever-changing artwork.

❊ Buy artist's palettes in a variety of shapes at an art and craft store. Use a flat brush to paint them with two coats of blackboard paint, allowing the paint to dry between coats.

❊ Hang the blackboards from the thumb holes on screws in the wall at a height that children can reach, or line them up on a worktop.

❊ Keep white or colored chalk and a blackboard eraser nearby to ensure regular use.

❊ To make the grouping of palette blackboards even more artistic, combine them with a well-used and colorful artist's palette.

ABC

9x

1 x 9 = 9
2 x 9 = 18
3 x 9 = 27
4 x 9 = 36
5 x 9 = 45
6 x 9 = 54
7 x 9 = 63
8 x 9 = 72
9 x 9 = 81
10 x 9 = 90

9x

5

𝍸𝍸 𝍸𝍸 𝍸𝍸

Illustrated notebooks

Personalize plain, utilitarian notebooks with illustrations that you know your child will love, to make books in which they can draw, write, or save favorite pictures they have cut out. If you give one to a child along with a new pen or set of pencils just before a vacation, they could use it as a travel journal. When children are older, they will enjoy looking back at the sweet notes and drawings as much as you will.

✳ Look out for old, dilapidated books, cards, or pictures at thrift stores, flea markets, and garage sales. They are usually inexpensive, but if you feel they are too precious to cut up you could color photocopy them and use the copies. You could also plunder old comics or simply print out images from the computer.

✳ Buy inexpensive notebooks with plain cardboard covers. Place a notebook over an illustration, taking care to position it correctly, and draw around the notebook lightly with a pencil. Take the book away and readjust the position if necessary, erasing the first lines. Cut out with a scalpel, metal ruler, and cutting mat or with scissors.

✳ Stick the cut-out illustration to the cover using a glue stick or double-sided tape applied right up to the edges. For longevity, you could cover the notebook with clear, self-adhesive vinyl. Also stick the occasional surprise inside the book—a small illustration that will delight your child when they stumble across it.

✳ Some of my notebooks already had fabric bindings on the spine, extending onto the front and back. On another, I stuck on my own fabric binding.

✳ Make bookmarks from ribbon, seam binding, or twill tape, cutting the ends with pinking shears.

QUICK IDEAS
Wishing board

It's natural for children always to be wishing for things, but this project encourages them to wish for things to do and places to see, rather than the latest toy or computer game. As they learn about the rest of the world, they can wish to visit a particular place and illustrate their wishes with its special features, whether it is the giant tortoises of the Galapagos Islands, an airplane to take them on their next vacation, or a sandcastle to make on a trip to the beach. Encourage children to think of simple wishes that don't cost money, such as watching the butterflies land on flowers in the park, picking strawberries for dessert, or scuffling through dry leaves in the fall. If they are getting frustrated waiting for something they are excited about like a birthday party, illustrating their wish with balloons, cake, or their friends playing games will feel as though they are doing something tangible to make it happen sooner. The Wishing Board is a wonderful visual diary of joyful anticipation.

✸ Cut an old, salvaged floorboard into three equal lengths and nail them to a piece of hardboard. Sand it down and whitewash the wood with watered-down white latex (emulsion) paint. Finally, hammer some nails partway into the wood to hang the wishes on. (Make sure the nails are the type with heads, to stop the tags containing the wishes from slipping off.)

✸ Assemble swing tags of different sizes, for children to draw on using a black fiber-tip pen.

✸ For added visual interest and color, glue little buttons to the heads of some of the nails and use small ribbons to hang the tags containing their wishes from these.

CHAPTER 4

To Wear

Reflect your child's personality in their clothes and accessories using these projects. Involve the child in choosing ribbons for shoelaces, drawing images or threading buttons for jewelry, picking out fabrics for a hair band or a collar neckpiece, or deciding on motifs to add to a sweater, a satchel, or a homemade badge. The only problem will be getting the child to take them off at bedtime.

Charm bracelet
and necklace

Drawing colored pictures on shrink plastic—a specialized plastic paper that magically shrinks, thickens, and hardens in the oven— and making them into charms is fabulous fun to do with children. You just can't help peering through the oven window and watching the paper curl up, reduce in size, and then flatten once more. As the drawings shrink, the color intensifies, too. I asked my children to draw pictures of fruit, Japanese dolls, and flowers in colored pencils on the plastic, then we added buttons, semiprecious stones, and beads for extra interest.

materials and equipment

Sheets of shrink plastic such as Shrinkies™ or Shrink Art™ in white or frosted (colored pencils can't be used on the clear type)

Colored pencils

Small, sharp scissors and hole punch

Oven and oven glove

Baking sheet and aluminum foil

Tweezers (optional)

Narrow ribbon

Sewing needle and thread to match ribbon

Embroidery needle and stranded floss (optional)

Small beads, buttons, and/or semiprecious stones

Toggle clasp or other type of jewelry clasp (for necklace)

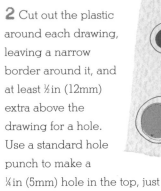

2 Cut out the plastic around each drawing, leaving a narrow border around it, and at least ½in (12mm) extra above the drawing for a hole. Use a standard hole punch to make a ¼in (5mm) hole in the top, just over ¼in (7mm) from the edge.

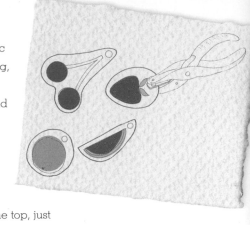

1 Ask the children to draw images on the rough side of the shrink plastic with colored pencils. Bear in mind that the images will shrink to about one-seventh of the size, so make sure the drawings aren't too small. Don't worry if the colors look weak; they will become stronger once the plastic has shrunk. Be sure to read the manufacturer's instructions before beginning.

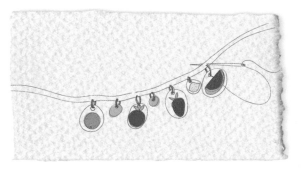

4 Cut the ribbon to the right length for your child's wrist or neck, depending on whether you are making a bracelet or necklace. The bracelet and necklace shown here are 12in (30cm) and 14½in (37cm) long respectively. Using a needle and thread or floss, sew the plastic charms to the central 5in (12.5cm) of the ribbon, interspersing the charms with beads, buttons, and/or semiprecious stones.

3 Preheat the oven to 325°F/170°C/gas mark 3, or the temperature recommended by the manufacturer. Put the shapes on a foil-lined baking sheet and place in the oven, making sure the children don't get too close. Bake the plastic shapes for a few minutes. They will curl up at first but will then uncurl, and they are ready when they are flat again. Remove the baking sheet using an oven glove. Leave to cool. If the shapes have curled up and stuck together, the oven may be too hot, so carefully separate the stuck edges using tweezers, and reheat in a slightly cooler oven.

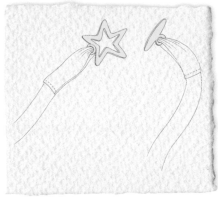

5 For a necklace, attach the two halves of a toggle clasp (an easy type of clasp for children to use) to the ribbon by pushing the ends of the ribbon through the holes in the two halves of the clasp, and sewing the ends in place on the underside of the ribbon.

TIP

You can also use this technique to make badges, fridge magnets, pencil toppers, and key fobs.

CHARM BRACELET AND NECKLACE

113

Button
family

The idea for this little button family came to me one day when all of my family was around me. The buttons can be mini portraits of your own family and pets, or characters from a story, or your children's favorite animals, and they can be sewn onto bags, pillows, or clothing. They are made by embroidering features onto small circles of fabric and then using these to cover button forms from covered-button kits. The embroidery isn't complicated, but if you prefer, you could draw the features using fabric pens instead (in which case you may wish to attach the buttons with safety pins in order to be able to remove the buttons prior to laundering).

materials and equipment

Pencil

Scraps of unbleached muslin or other cotton in white and/or beige

Covered-button kits in assorted sizes

Embroidery needle and floss in red, pink, and black (or colors of your choice)

Small, sharp scissors

Sewing needle and matching thread

Embroidery needle and crewel yarn

Narrow ribbon and tiny beads

Fabric carrier bag or pillow cover

Fabric scraps in black and beige (for animal family—see Tip)

1 For each face, use a pencil to draw on the white fabric a circle to the size specified in the kit. Place the button-form in the center and draw around it very faintly. Draw in the features on this face very lightly. Repeat for all the other "family members."

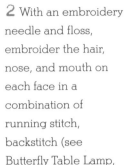
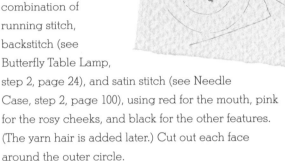

2 With an embroidery needle and floss, embroider the hair, nose, and mouth on each face in a combination of running stitch, backstitch (see Butterfly Table Lamp, step 2, page 24), and satin stitch (see Needle Case, step 2, page 100), using red for the mouth, pink for the rosy cheeks, and black for the other features. (The yarn hair is added later.) Cut out each face around the outer circle.

3 Using sewing thread, hand sew a gathering thread around the outside of each circle, leaving long ends. Place the button-form upside-down in the center on the wrong side of the circle, and pull both ends of the thread so that it gathers up around the button; tie the ends. Make sure that the face is straight to the shank, otherwise it will be at an angle when the button is sewn on.

4 Stretch the fabric over the button-form so that it catches on the tiny hooks inside the button-form. Smooth out any bumps, then press the back plate into the button-form.

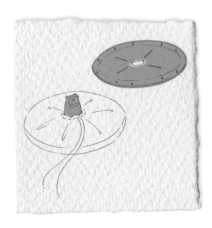

5 For the girl's hair above the braids, thread a long length of crewel yarn through the embroidery needle and knot the end. Bring the needle from the back and through the girl's head at the center of the top edge. Insert the needle from the front halfway down the side, making one long stitch on the head. Make a few more long stitches next to each other on one side of the girl's head, then repeat on the other side of her head. For each braid, knot another length of yarn and insert the needle from the back at ear level. Leaving a loop, make a small stitch at the ear, then repeat two more times. Cut the loops at the bottom, and then braid the six strands (two at a time). Tie the end of each braid with narrow ribbon.

6 Make the mother's hair in the same way but have several shorter loops on each side and don't cut or braid them. To create her necklace, thread tiny beads onto a double length of sewing thread, and sew the ends to the back at the bottom edge.

7 Sew the buttons in place on a fabric bag or pillow cover, using a double length of sewing thread.

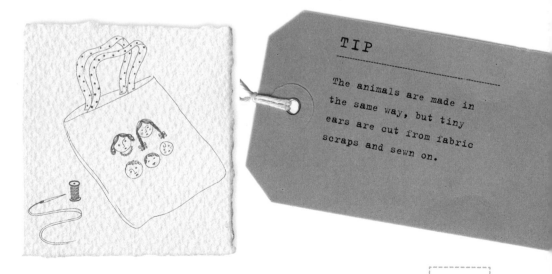

TIP

The animals are made in the same way, but tiny ears are cut from fabric scraps and sewn on.

Flower hair band
and clips

Most little girls love wearing hair accessories, especially when the items are homemade. These hair clips and hair band are decorated with padded fabric flowers, made from scraps of fabric in an eclectic mix of patterns. I chose small, ditzy prints, polka-dots, and even some metallic fabric, all of which came from my box of tiny scraps and remnants. If you are making a skirt or dress for a child, you could perhaps make a hair clip or band to match, or even just use the fabric for one or two leaves to tie the outfit together subtly. You could also make these fabric flowers into brooches, bracelets, or other jewelry.

materials and equipment

Compass (optional) and pencil

Ruler and small, sharp scissors

Fabric scraps

Sewing needle and matching thread

Batting (wadding)

Embroidery needle and stranded floss

Fusible web

Iron and ironing board

Stiff hair band

Double-sided tape, for hair band

Strong cotton thread

Hair clips

Clear-drying all-purpose glue such as UHU, for hair clips

Flower

1 For one flower, draw a circle about 3¼ in (8cm) in diameter on the wrong side of the fabric. (Either use a compass or draw around something of the right size, such as the inside of a roll of masking tape.) Cut out the circle. With a sewing needle and thread, sew running stitch around the circle about ¼ in (5mm) from the edge, leaving long ends.

2 Pull the ends of the thread to gather up the circle. Place some batting (wadding) inside, and then pull the threads tight to close up the hole, and knot the ends.

3 Thread an embroidery needle with a long length of floss (using all six strands); knot one end. Insert the needle into the padded circle through the hole, which will be at the back, and bring it out at center front. Take the needle over the edge and insert it again through the hole at center back and bring it out again at center front, pulling it tight. This time, take it over the edge at the opposite side of the circle before once again inserting it at center back. Continue in the same way until you have divided the flower into eight equal segments using the floss, pulling it tight each time. Secure the floss at the back.

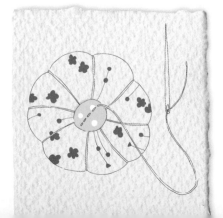

4 Cut out a ⅜ in (1cm) circle from a different fabric scrap and sew it to the center front with a sewing needle and thread.

5 Iron fusible web to the wrong side of one fabric scrap, remove the backing paper, and iron this to the wrong side of another fabric scrap. Draw and cut out two leaf shapes from this. Sew them to the back of the padded flower, so that each of the two fabrics is at the front of one leaf and at the back of the other leaf.

Hair band

1 For the hair band, stick double-sided tape along the outside of the hair band. Cut a long strip of fabric about 1¼in (3cm) wide, and press under a narrow hem along one long edge and one end. Stick that end of the strip to one end of the band, and wind the strip around the band so that the turned-under edge covers the raw edge as you work your way around. Trim off any excess fabric, turn under the end, and stick in place with more tape.

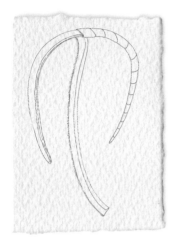

2 Make three flowers. Use a sewing needle and strong cotton thread to sew each one to the fabric on the band, and then wind the thread around and around the band to hold it tightly in place. Now cut three narrow strips of fabric about 4in (10cm) long. Leaving the edges of the strips raw, tie each around the headband to cover the wound thread beneath each flower.

Hair clips

Make one flower for each hair clip, and attach to the clip using a sewing needle and strong cotton thread. Make secure stitches at the back of the flower, wind the thread around both sides of the clip, then fasten the thread at the back of the flower. Use a little glue to stop the flower sliding down the clip.

Cloud
sweater

Transforming a simple, **classic piece of clothing into something special** and unique that will appeal to a young child is surprisingly easy. Here, some basic appliqué and embroidery have turned a child's plain V-neck sweater into a top that any little boy or girl will love. Running-stitch detail is added to the neck, waistband, and cuffs, but you can also add other embroidered detailing, such as the **child's initials** at the back or **a little rainbow** above the waistband. To finish it off, I replaced the manufacturer's label with a polka-dot ribbon and added a hanging loop made from striped tape, plus two small buttons.

materials and equipment

Fusible web

Iron and ironing board

Plain cream-colored wool-mix fabric

Pins

Pattern for cloud (see page 184)

Small, sharp scissors

Child's sweater

Embroidery needle and stranded floss in color to match sweater and in cream

Batting (wadding)

3¼in (8.5cm) length of striped ribbon or tape, ⅜in (1cm) wide

5½in (14cm) length of polka-dot ribbon, ½–¾in (1.5–2cm) wide

Sewing needle and thread to match sweater

2 small buttons

1 Iron fusible web to the wrong side of the cream fabric. You won't be ironing it to the sweater, but the fusible web will stiffen the fabric, keep the edges crisp, and prevent raveling. Pin the cloud pattern to the fabric, and cut around it.

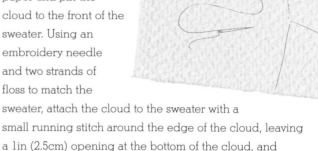

2 Remove the backing paper and pin the cloud to the front of the sweater. Using an embroidery needle and two strands of floss to match the sweater, attach the cloud to the sweater with a small running stitch around the edge of the cloud, leaving a 1in (2.5cm) opening at the bottom of the cloud, and fastening off the threads at the ends.

3 Stuff batting (wadding) behind the cloud through the opening, and then sew up the gap with the same small running stitch and floss as you used around the rest of the cloud.

TIP

Although running stitch is the simplest of all line stitches, you can vary the effect by altering the size of the stitches, distance between them, and thickness (determined by the number of strands you use). For tiny stitches, use no more than two strands.

4 Using the embroidery needle and three strands of cream floss, embroider vertical lines of running stitch beneath the cloud to create the raindrops. The vertical lines should be different lengths.

5 Also embroider tiny running stitches around the V-neck using two strands of cream floss (stitching just through the top layer of the band, so the stitching doesn't show inside the neckline), and along the top edge of the waistband using three strands of cream floss. On one or both cuffs, sew about six lines of tiny running stitches parallel to the ribbing and very close together, using two strands of cream floss.

6 With small, sharp scissors, carefully cut off the manufacturer's label at the back of the neck, and remove it. Turn under ⅛in (3mm) at each end of the piece of striped ribbon or tape, and sew the ends securely to the inside of the neck, with a gap of about ⅝in (1.5cm) between them, to form a decorative hanging loop. Turn under ¼in (5mm) on the ends of the polka-dot ribbon and sew this over the ends of the loop, replacing the manufacturer's label.

7 On the outside of the back neck, sew on two small buttons, positioning them over the ends of the hanging loop that are on the inside.

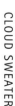

Bird
brooch

This sweet little brooch will liven up any little girl's coat. The **robin's red breast adds a splash of color,** or for a more subtle look you can use red stitching to represent it instead—both versions are pictured here. In fact, if you made both styles, facing in opposite directions, the two birds could be worn together to keep each other company. Or you could use the same technique to make a **colorful parrot brooch from bright-colored felt.** The robin could be worn in winter and the parrot in summer.

materials and equipment

Fusible web

Iron and ironing board

Scraps of felt in cream and red

Pins and small, sharp scissors

Pattern for bird (see page 184)

Sewing needle and thread in cream, black, and red

Sequin or tiny button

Brooch back

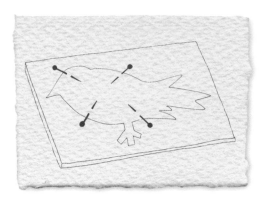

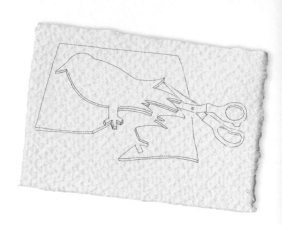

1 Following the manufacturer's instructions, iron fusible web to the back of the cream felt and the red felt. Pin the bird pattern on the front of the cream felt and cut out the shape.

2 Remove the backing paper from the fusible web and iron the bird shape to another piece of cream felt. Cut out the shape as closely as possible to the first bird shape.

3 Using the bird pattern, cut out a wing from the cream felt and a breast from the red felt. Remove the backing paper, and iron the breast to the front of the cream bird.

4 With a sewing needle and cream thread, sew running stitch around the outside edge of the bird. Attach the wing with a cross stitch in black thread near the front corner only, to allow it to flap. Sew on a sequin or tiny button for the eye. On the reverse side of the bird, sew on a brooch back.

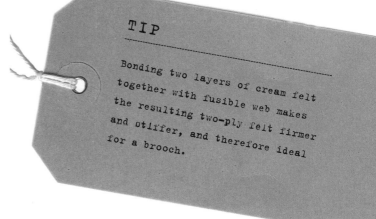

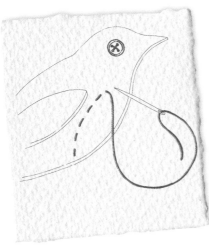

5 Make a second bird by reversing the pattern and repeating steps 1–4 but omitting the red breast. With a sewing needle and red thread, sew running stitch along the upper edge of the breast.

TIP

Bonding two layers of cream felt together with fusible web makes the resulting two-ply felt firmer and stiffer, and therefore ideal for a brooch.

Fun
satchel

Practical and fun, this canvas satchel is the perfect accompaniment for a child's day out. Not only will it hold snacks and sandwiches, but it is also large enough for found treasures like pebbles and feathers. Every child will love the personalized luggage label, with their initials or name on one side and a star on the other, while some of the other decorations could perhaps be earned as rewards. For example, a child coming first, second, or third place in, say, a running race could receive a badge with the appropriate number on it. The stripes on the straps could be added one at a time for good behavior or doing well at school, rather like military stripes.

materials and equipment

Ribbons and tapes in assorted widths and colors

Small, sharp scissors

For each badge, one covered-button kit for button about 1½in (4cm) in diameter

Scraps of fabric including striped fabric

Sewing needle and matching thread

Iron and ironing board

Fusible web

Safety pins

Army surplus canvas satchel

Two 10in (25cm) squares of fabric in yellow and gray (or colors of your choice)

Compass and pencil

4½in (11.5cm) square of linen fabric

Hole punch

1yd (1m) ribbon, ⅛in (3mm) wide, to match satchel

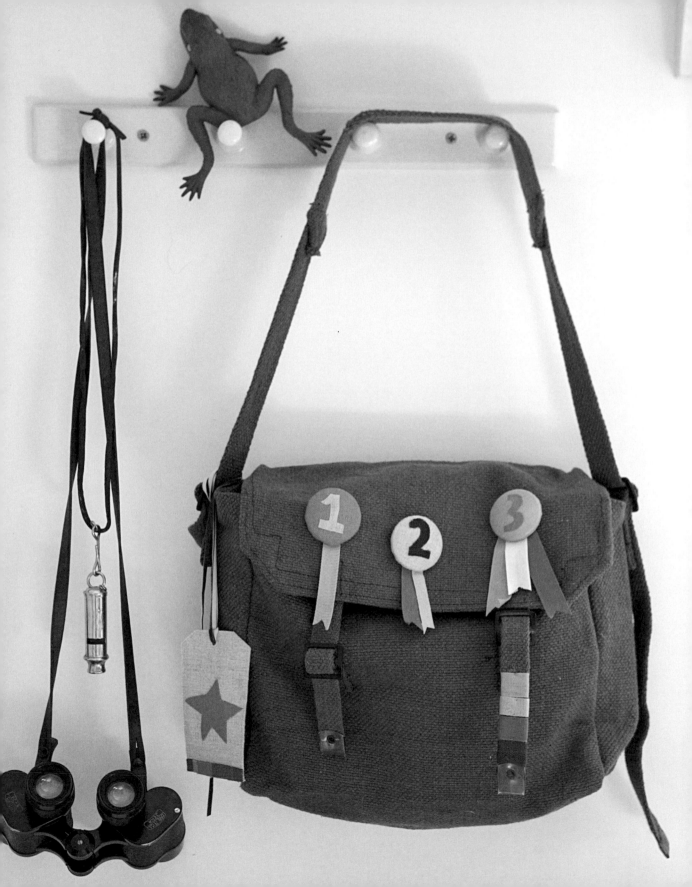

Badges

1 For each badge, cut up to three 2–3in (6–8cm) lengths of ribbons and tapes in different colors, cutting a V-shape into one end of each. Following the manufacturer's instructions, cover a button-form with a circle of fabric (see Button Family, steps 1, 3, and 4, page 116), sandwiching the straight ends of up to three pieces of ribbon between the front and back sections of the button-form before pushing the back into place. Repeat to make as many badges as you wish.

2 Following the manufacturer's instructions, iron fusible web to the back of some fabric scraps in different colors that contrast with the covered buttons. Make sure there will be enough left over to use later for the label letters and bull's-eye and star (see opposite). On the backing paper of each, draw a number in reverse. Cut it out, remove the backing, and iron one onto each covered button. Attach a safety pin to the back of each badge, and pin onto the flap of the satchel.

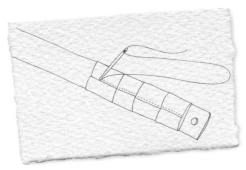

Stripy strap

Cut four pieces of ribbon in different colors, each to a length of twice the width of the strap, plus ½in (1cm). Wrap one piece tightly around one of the front straps, turning under the ends on the underside and sewing them together. Repeat to attach another piece so it butts up against the first. Attach the remaining pieces in the same way.

Bull's-eye and star

1 Iron fusible web to the wrong side of two 10in (25cm) fabric squares in yellow and gray (or colors of your choice). Using a compass and pencil, draw an 8in (20cm) circle on the yellow one (placing it close to a corner of the square) and a 5½in (14cm) circle on the gray one. Cut out both circles. In the center of the gray circle, cut out a 3¼in (8.5cm) circle. Save the gray circle to use for the star on the label (see opposite).

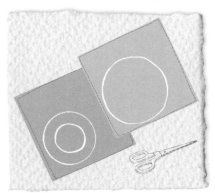

2 Remove the backing paper from the gray ring, place it centrally on the yellow circle, and iron in place. Now remove the backing from the yellow circle and iron this centrally to the back of the satchel. Draw and cut out a star from the leftover yellow fabric, remove the backing, and iron this alongside. Draw and cut out another star from one of the leftover scraps that you backed with fusible web for the badges (see Badges, step 2, opposite) and apply in the same way to the center of the bull's-eye. Using matching thread, sew around the edges of the shapes to attach them more securely.

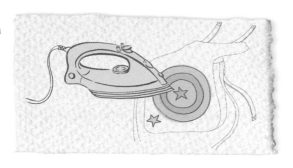

Label

1 Cut the 4½in (11.5cm) square of linen fabric in half. Iron fusible web to the wrong side of one half, remove the backing, and iron this to the other half to create a thick, stiff rectangle of fabric. Cut off the corners at one end, creating a luggage-label shape. Make a hole in the top of the linen fabric label using a hole punch.

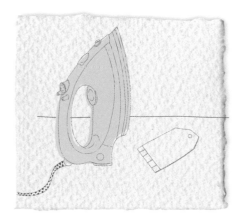

2 Iron fusible web to the back of the striped fabric, and cut two narrow strips with the length running across the stripes at right angles to make them multicolored. Remove the backing and iron one strip to each side of the label, along the side or bottom edge.

3 Draw and cut out a star and some initials from the scraps of fabric you have already backed with fusible web, remove backing, and iron onto the front and back of the label. Fold the ⅛in- (3mm-) wide ribbon in half and insert the loop through the hole in the top. Thread both ends through the loop. Tie the label to the main strap using this ribbon.

Reversible
collar neckpiece

This reversible collar is a fun, simple way to give a dress, a top, or even a T-shirt a new look and a splash of color and pattern. A different, but coordinating, pattern is used for the other side of the collar, making it even more versatile. It also looks sweet worn with the bow tied at the front rather than the back. You could make the collar from two small fabric remnants, and if you have some fabric left over from a skirt you have made, you could then give a top a collar that matches the skirt.

materials and equipment

Pattern for collar (see page 186)

Small remnants of two coordinating fabrics, such as polka-dot and floral

Pins

Dressmaking shears and small, sharp scissors

Sewing machine and thread to match fabrics

24in (60cm) length of ribbon at least 1/8in (1cm) wide

Iron and ironing board

Sewing needle and thread to match ribbon

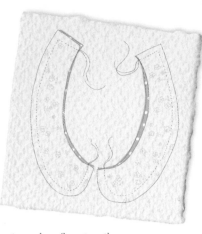

2 With right sides together, pin one collar shape to its mirror image in the other fabric. Machine stitch a ⅜in (1cm) seam around the outer edge (leaving the inner edge unstitched), pivoting at the corner (see Tip) if you are having corners, and making the curves as smooth as possible. Repeat to join the other two collar shapes to each other.

1 With this pattern, you can have square corners at the back of the collar or rounded-off corners. Fold one piece of fabric in half, and pin the pattern to it (not on the fold). Cut around the pattern, to give two collar shapes. Remove the pattern, and repeat for the other piece of fabric. You now have four collar shapes, two of them the mirror images of the other two.

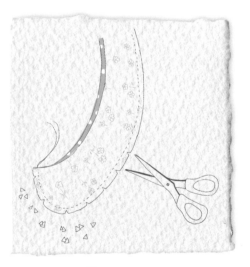

3 Trim the seam allowances to ¼in (5mm), and snip into the seam allowances on the curves, being careful not to snip through the actual stitching. Also snip off the point of the seam allowance at the corner if your collar has corners.

4 Turn the collar pieces right side out, push out any corners so they are sharp, and press.

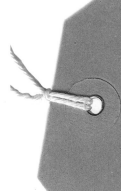

TIP

To stitch around a corner, mark the corner (the point where the two seam lines will cross). Stitch up to the corner, stopping with the needle in the fabric. Raise the presser foot and turn the fabric until the new seam line is exactly in front of the needle—this is called a pivot. Now lower the presser foot and continue stitching.

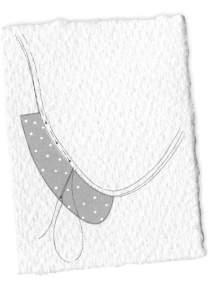

5 Fold the ribbon in half lengthwise and slot it over the raw edge of one collar piece so that the deeper end of the collar piece is at the center of the ribbon. Pin through all four layers. Using a thread that matches the ribbon, hand sew the ribbon inconspicuously to the outside of the collar, then sew the other edge of the ribbon to the inside of the collar in the same way.

6 Attach the other collar piece to the remainder of the ribbon in the same way, with the curved edge meeting that of the first collar at the center of the ribbon.

137

REVERSIBLE COLLAR NECKPIECE

Button jewelry

This fun and colorful jewelry is simplicity itself to make. Buttons are strung onto a bright-colored leather thong, which not only adds color but also is strong enough not to break. Because the leather thong is easy to thread with buttons, your children can help with the process.

✹ Raid your button box for lots of buttons of a similar size, and try to choose colors that will work well together. Choose a leather thong that goes with these colors and cut it to the desired length for a necklace or bracelet. Tie a loose knot at one end, and thread the buttons onto it.

✹ When you have finished, hold up both ends of the leather thong, allowing the buttons to fall to the center. Undo the loose knot, tie a knot at one end of the buttons and then another at the other end of the buttons (keeping the ends of the leather thong of equal length) to stop the buttons from sliding around.

Fun hankies

These colorful hankies are so jolly that you'll have no difficulty persuading a child to get in the habit of using hankies rather than their sleeve! Choose a cotton that has a novelty print such as children's motifs, or a fine cotton lawn in a pretty print, or a solid-color cotton that you can decorate. For each hanky, cut a square of fabric about 10–12in (25–32cm) square, and either press a narrow hem all around and hand sew or machine stitch it, or just finish the raw edges with a small zigzag stitch or by overlocking the edge if your machine can do that.

✳ Decorate a solid-color hanky or a pretty lace-trimmed vintage hanky with appliqué. Simply iron fusible web to the back of a novelty fabric, cut out some motifs from the backed fabric, remove the backing paper from the fusible web, and then iron the motifs to the hanky, following the manufacturer's instructions. To help it withstand frequent laundering, you can finish by machining a narrow zigzag stitch, or hand embroidering a small running stitch, around the edges of the motifs.

✳ Cut out one or more short pieces of colorful ribbon or seam binding, turn under the ends, fold the pieces in half, and stitch the ends to the edge of a hanky to add interest.

✳ Personalize a hanky by embroidering the child's initials with machine satin (or zigzag) stitch.

Ribbon shoelaces

This is a really simple idea that will work on a baby's first shoes, a teenager's sneakers, or even your own shoes! It is an easy way to add flashes of bright color to an outfit, customize your child's clothing, and allow them to show some individuality. The ribbon can match an outfit for a special occasion, contrast with it vividly, or simply be the child's favorite color. Solid-colored, striped, polka-dot, or lace ribbons will all work. The laces don't even need to match—children will love using a different color on each shoe.

✳ Remove one of the original laces and use it as your guide to the length of the ribbons, then cut each ribbon about ½in (1cm) longer. (Sometimes laces are a bit too short to tie properly, so this is your opportunity to make them the right length.) On a wider ribbon, it may be necessary to cut the ends at an angle to allow them to be poked through the holes in the shoes.

✳ Use the shoe that still has the original lace in it as a guide to lacing up the other shoe with one ribbon— these days, shoes may be laced up in all sorts of unconventional ways, which affect the length that is needed. Now remove the remaining original lace and lace up that shoe with the second ribbon.

✳ Finally, turn under ¼in (5mm) at each end, and stitch so that they won't ravel. If it is a non-raveling type of ribbon, this isn't necessary.

CHAPTER 5 # Storage

The key to a tidy home is effective storage. In this chapter you'll find storage ideas that are not just practical but also decorative, from treasure jars and paint cans covered with stamps to stenciled vintage suitcases. Projects like the curiosity cabinet and the bookcase dollhouse are a combination of functional and fun, but all the projects will help you keep the children's toys under control.

Curiosity
cabinet

This old cabinet used to hang on my bedroom wall when I was a child, but it was dark and heavy-looking, so I freshened it up with paint to match my daughter's bedroom decor. Its **glass doors make it ideal for displaying a child's prized possessions** and curiosities. To add to the sense of wonder it creates, I've added vases of flowers—but the vases are painted on the inside back and their flowers are made from lace and floral fabric. Coupled with the real vases placed in front of them, holding silk flowers and genuine blooms, they **create an amusing ambiguity** over just what is real and what is not.

materials and equipment

Old wooden cabinet with glass doors

Sugar soap, water, and sponge, or fine sandpaper (optional)

Old newspaper and scrap paper

Masking tape

Undercoat

Flat paintbrushes, ½in (1.5cm) and 1¼in (3cm) wide

Water- or oil-based eggshell paint in white or off-white and colors of your choice

Tape measure and pencil

Frisket masking film in matte finish (see Spotty Dotty Chairs, Tip, page 93)

Craft knife and cutting mat

Pattern for flower (see page 186)

Stiff, flat brush, ½in (1.5cm) wide

Tester pots of latex (emulsion) paints in colors of your choice

Fusible web or fusible interfacing

Iron and ironing board

Scraps of floral fabric, and of lace fabric with floral motifs (if possible)

Small, sharp scissors

White glue

1 Remove the shelves if possible. If necessary, sand the cabinet or clean it inside and out with sugar soap, water, and a sponge, leaving it to dry on newspaper. Apply masking tape to the glass along all the edges to protect it from the paint. Apply undercoat inside and out, using a ½in (1.5cm) flat brush between the panes of glass and a 1¼in (3cm) flat brush for the rest. Leave to dry. Now paint the interior in white or off-white, and the shelves and exterior in the same or in colors of your choice, leaving it to dry after each coat. You may need to apply several coats. When the final coat is dry or nearly dry, carefully remove the masking tape.

2 Put the shelves back in, in the desired positions, allowing room for taller items such as real vases and books. Measure the height of the shelves, and on scrap paper draw some vase shapes that will

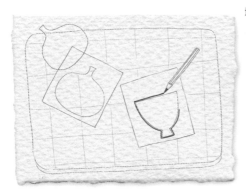

fit in these spaces (allowing for them to hold flowers, if desired). After sketching each vase, cut it out, fold it in half, and trim the two layers together to make the vase symmetrical. Draw around the vases on Frisket masking film (see Tip, page 93). Cut out using a craft knife and cutting mat, discarding the vase shapes to leave stencils with vase-shaped windows. Using the flower pattern, make a flower stencil in the same way, to use with one of the vases.

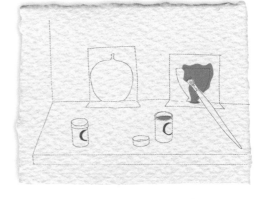

3 Place the stencils against the back of the cabinet, taking time to create the most attractive arrangement, and then press the self-adhesive backs in place; the bottom of the stencil will be stuck to the shelf, so that the window in the stencil is flush with the shelf. Using a ½in (1.5cm) stiff, flat brush, apply paint from a tester pot in your chosen color, painting within the stencil window and brushing away from its edges. Leave to dry and then apply a second coat and allow to dry. Remove the stencils. (If two vases are very close together, it's easier to stencil both coats for one vase, allowing the paint to dry after each coat, and then remove the stencil before starting on the adjacent one.)

4 For a polka-dot vase, stick the vase stencil in position, and then cut out small circles from the Frisket film and stick these in place within the stencil window before applying the paint. Alternatively, simply apply dots of paint in the same color as the background after the stenciled vase has dried.

5 Iron fusible web or interfacing to the wrong side of the floral fabric to stiffen it, and then cut out a flower-and-leaf-spray motif. Remove the backing paper from the fusible web, if used, and apply white glue to the web or interfacing side of the flower-and-leaf spray. Stick it in place above a vase.

TIP

If you don't have a suitable cabinet, try this idea on a wall above a shelf, chest of drawers, or cupboard.

6 Cut out a floral motif from the lace fabric (or cut out a flower shape if the lace does not have floral motifs). Apply glue to the wrong side, and stick it in place above another vase.

Bookcase
dollhouse

This is inspired by a dollhouse my father made for me when I was a child. It makes **a wonderful birthday gift** that will be treasured for years to come. Use an old or inexpensive bookcase, and have fun decorating it—if it isn't a surprise present, involve the child in the process or in the choice of colors. It could be a **mini version of your house** or you could try a quirky color scheme. Tester pots of paint, and samples or remnants of wallpapers, fabrics, and carpets will enable you to decorate it for next to nothing. It could also provide **storage for books and small boxes,** slipped in among the furniture. When the child is too old for a dollhouse, you could replace the furniture with books—though you may meet with some resistance from a sentimental child!

materials and equipment

Bookcase consisting of at least two shelves

Water, sugar soap, and newspaper; or fine sandpaper (all optional)

Undercoat

Flat paintbrushes, 1¼in (3cm) and ½in (1.5cm) wide

Latex (emulsion) paint in white or off-white

Tester pots of latex (emulsion) paint in assorted colors, including a dark shade

Artist's paintbrush, size 5

Pencil, metal ruler, and general-purpose scissors

Wallpaper samples and remnants

Cutting mat and craft knife

White glue and brush

Cartridge paper

Old watch faces and small mirrors

Adhesive pads

Scraps of fabrics and carpet

Dollhouse furniture

1 Wash the bookcase with water and sugar soap, and leave to dry on newspaper; or sand it down and then wipe clean, as necessary. Paint it all over with undercoat using a 1¼in (3cm) flat brush. When dry, paint with white or off-white latex (emulsion); leave to dry. Paint the top and front of the top shelf in a dark color, to suggest a roof.

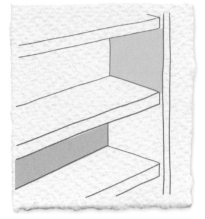

2 Decide which inside "walls" are to be painted which colors, and paint them with a ½in (1.5cm) flat brush, taking care not to go over the edges unless the adjacent wall is one you will be wallpapering. Touch up any mistakes with some paint and an artist's brush. Leave to dry.

3 Measure the "walls" you will be papering, mark out pieces of wallpaper to those dimensions, and then cut out using a cutting mat, metal ruler, and craft knife. Check that the wallpaper will fit, adjusting the size if

necessary, and also check that you are happy with how it will look. Paint white glue onto the back of one piece and stick it in place, smoothing out any air bubbles. Repeat for the other pieces of wallpaper.

4 You could create your own pattern by cutting out individual flowers from a floral wallpaper and gluing them onto a painted wall, as I have done.

5 On cartridge paper, draw a door with several panels and a fanlight and draw some windows with windowpanes. Paint the lines using the dark color you used for the roof and an artist's paintbrush. When the outlines are dry, paint on some colorful curtains at the windows. Leave to dry, then cut out the door and windows with scissors, and paint some white glue onto the backs using a brush. Stick in place on the outside of the bookcase. You could also make a door and windows for the inside in the same way and glue them in positions corresponding to the ones on the outside.

6 Stick old watch faces and small mirrors to the walls with adhesive pads. Cut pieces of fabric or old carpet to the right size for rugs or wall-to-wall carpets, and glue in place; allow to dry. When the house is decorated, add miniature furniture, which you could paint first if you wish, to match the color schemes.

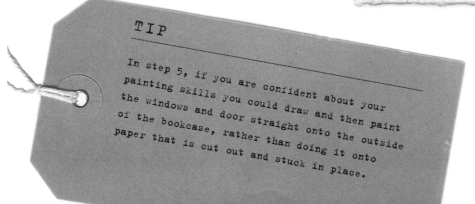

TIP

In step 5, if you are confident about your painting skills you could draw and then paint the windows and door straight onto the outside of the bookcase, rather than doing it onto paper that is cut out and stuck in place.

Vintage
suitcase storage

Old suitcases in a wide range of sizes can frequently be found at flea markets. Some are beautiful just as they are, but those that are badly scratched or slightly damaged are perfect for a revamp, particularly as they are often reasonably priced and excellent for storage purposes. My children keep their drawings safe and flat in one suitcase. **Another case holds all their pencils,** and others keep paints, brushes, and craft supplies in order. Toy cars and train sets, dolls, and building blocks can also all be stored in these versatile cases. As an attractive way of labeling them, use stenciling and decoupage to depict the contents, as with the pencil decoration shown here.

materials and equipment

Old suitcases in various sizes

Frisket masking film in matte finish (See Spotty Dotty Chairs, Tip, page 93)

Pencil

Craft knife and cutting mat

Water- or oil-based eggshell paints in assorted colors for background colors

Stiff, flat paintbrushes, 1in (2.5cm) and ½in (1.5cm) wide

Watercolor paper

Acrylic or latex (emulsion) paints in assorted colors, including gray

Metal ruler

Pinking shears (optional)

Two fine artist's paintbrushes

White glue

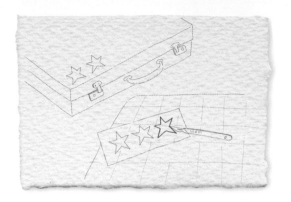

1 To allow some of the original suitcase to show through, such as the brown leather on the blue suitcase shown here, do some reverse stenciling. Draw shapes such as stars or hearts on matte Frisket masking film (see Tip, page 93), and cut out the shapes using a craft knife and cutting mat. Save the surround from one of the shapes to use in step 7, and stick the Frisket shapes in position on the suitcase (Frisket is self-adhesive).

2 With the Frisket shapes in place, paint the outside of the suitcase (apart from the bottom) using a 1in (2.5cm) flat brush, taking particular care around the fastenings and handle—use a ½in (1.5cm) flat brush around them to make it easier to control the paint. Leave to dry, and then turn the suitcase over and paint the bottom. When dry, apply a second coat in the same way. When the paint is dry or nearly dry, carefully peel off the Frisket shapes.

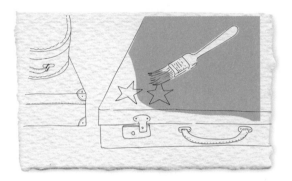

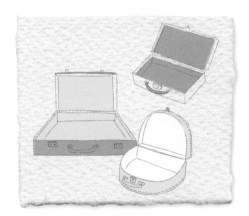

3 Paint the inside of the suitcase with two coats of a contrasting color, allowing the paint to dry after each coat. If there is a natural line, such as stitching or the edge of the case, paint up to that line. Paint the handle the same color as the suitcase exterior or interior, or a contrasting color—or leave it natural if you prefer.

4 For the pencils, use a flat ½in (1.5cm) brush to paint watercolor paper with blocks of paint in gray and bright colors that contrast with the suitcase paint (one bright color for each pencil). When dry, use a craft knife, metal ruler, and cutting mat to cut out strips of the same size, one of each color. If you have pinking shears, use them to cut one zigzag end on each. For the erasers at the other ends, cut the gray strip into small rectangles of the same width as the other strips. From the unpainted part of the paper, cut out a triangle for each pencil to the same width.

5 With a fine artist's brush, paint white glue onto the underside of one strip, one gray eraser, and one white triangle. Stick them in position on the suitcase so that the ends butt up with each other. Repeat for the other

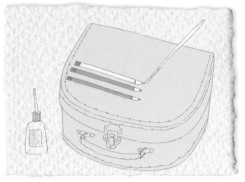

pencils. With a different artist's brush, paint the tip of each white triangle with the color of the pencil, to represent the pencil lead.

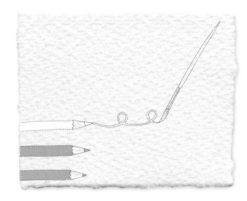

6 When the painted tips are dry, brush glue over the top of the paper pencils and just over their edges, to form a varnish that helps prevent them from peeling off. Using a fine paintbrush and the same color of paint as the pencil, paint a loopy line to represent handwriting coming from the pencil.

7 On the inside of the lid, stick the Frisket film surround from which you cut one of the shapes in step 2. Use the stiff, flat ½in (1.5cm) brush to paint a bright color through the window(s) in this stencil, to echo the shapes on the outside. When the paint is dry or nearly dry, remove the stencil.

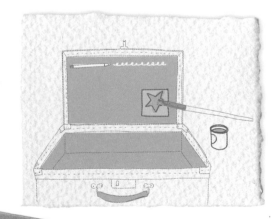

TIP

If you will be stacking suitcases of a similar size, have the reverse-stenciled shapes on the same side as the handle so that they remain visible when other suitcases are stacked on top.

VINTAGE SUITCASE STORAGE

Graphic boxes

Vintage wooden printer's trays were once used for storing individual letters employed in typesetting. They make wonderful containers for graphic displays while also helping children learn the basics of the alphabet, numbers, shapes, and colors. To fill these trays, I haunted collectors' fairs, craft stores and stationery suppliers, collecting and buying old metal and wooden letters and numerals, old board games with interesting counters, plus newspaper and magazine articles with interesting typefaces—the more varied the selection, the more interesting it will look. Printer's trays are often dark and dirty, so give them a good wash. Once dry, apply undercoat and several coats of white flat eggshell or latex (emulsion) paint, using a 1in (2.5cm) brush and allowing the paint to dry between coats.

❋ A large tray with at least 26 sections will allow you to display the alphabet and possibly also some numbers. Paint any that won't show up well, then stick in place with strong double-sided tape.

❋ Paint the sections of small trays in bright shades, and fill them with found treasures or wooden toys. I glued pieces of old maps to the fronts of wooden shapes to add interest. Stick all of these to the tray with strong double-sided tape.

❋ Paint the top side of a small printer's try to look like a roof, add a cardboard chimney, and turn two sections into a door and a window for a miniature dollhouse (pictured on page 2).

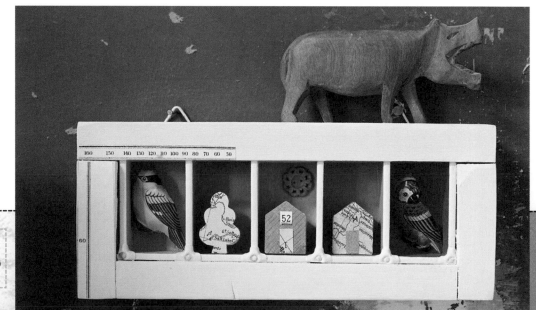

Put all those old glass jars to good use as decorative containers for your children's nature collections. They are ideal for shells, pebbles, sea glass, feathers, dead insects, and other souvenirs of days spent at the beach or exploring nature. Instead of being scattered all over the house, the treasure trove is contained in a neat system. The clear glass allows items to be admired and the labeling provides an attractive record of the jar's contents.

✲ Give the jars and lids a wash, scrubbing off the labels and glue in soapy water. Working in a well-ventilated area, with your work surface covered with newspaper, spray paint all the lids white, giving them a few light coats. When dry, stencil a black number on each lid.

QUICK IDEAS
Treasure jars

✲ For the labels, save the swing tags when you buy clothing, then cover the writing with plain stickers (or glue paper on top) so children can write on their own information, such as when and where the items were found. For other labels, cut out pieces of canvas, paint them white, then stamp numbers on the labels in black ink. You could also simply use luggage labels. Tie a label around the rim of each jar with string.

✲ Another idea is to cut a piece of canvas as deep as the jar's height and a little wider than the jar's circumference. Wrap it around the jar, overlapping the ends, and stick in place with double-sided tape.

As children get older, their games and toys seem to have more and more little bits and pieces to them, so storage is key to keeping order. If the storage is good-looking as well as functional, then it can be left out on display. I bought new, unused cans cheaply from a paint store, but if you want to reuse old paint cans, those that had contained water-based paint, such as latex (emulsion), will be easier to remove all traces of paint from. Make sure the lids are undamaged. The maps I covered these cans with were from an out-of-date atlas, but you can use maps relating to where you live, have been on vacation, or would like to visit.

QUICK IDEAS
Paint can storage

✷ Measure the height between top and bottom rims and circumference of each can, adding ½in (1cm) to the circumference for overlap. Cut out a rectangle to this size. Stick double-sided tape to each short edge and at least two more strips in between them. Peel the backing from the first strip, and stick that edge of the map along the can's vertical seam, making sure it is straight. Wrap the map around the can, removing the tape's backing as you go. Varnish the paper if you wish, leaving it to dry. Before putting the lid on, place under it a looped ribbon with knotted ends—to remove the lid, give the loop a tug.

✷ To make a moneybox with a slot in the lid, drill several holes next to each other until the slot is large enough for coins to fit through. Bend any rough edges and file them smooth to make it safe for little fingers.

CHAPTER 6

Outside

Give children an outside play space and they are happy. They will love growing plants in customized crates, using their own colorful garden chairs, or arranging alphabet pebbles. Some projects, such as the picnic blanket stenciled with animal tracks or the twirling ribbon sticks, can be taken to a park or beach to be enjoyed, while the clothesline playhouse will be a favorite for years.

Clothesline playhouse

A playhouse always sparks creative play, which is even better when combined with fresh air. This Clothesline Playhouse also provides shade on a hot day and a quiet place in which to read or draw. It makes a great hideaway, too, where supplies can be squirreled away. One of the windows is a pocket where toys, books, and pencils can be stashed. The playhouse can be as elaborate as you wish—for example, one side could be more detailed than the other, or you could use fabric pens rather than stitching to create the windows and doors. On a rainy day the playhouse can be brought indoors and draped over a broom handle placed between sturdy pieces of furniture.

materials and equipment

Set square (or a large magazine or book), tape measure, and long ruler

Pencil and pins

51in- (130cm-) wide fabric for house walls

Fabric for roof

Dressmaker's shears and small, sharp scissors

Iron and ironing board

Sewing machine and thread to match fabrics

Tailor's chalk

Paper for pattern

White felt and matching thread

Rickrack

Fusible web

Fabrics for windows and doors

Ribbons for windowpanes and rosettes

Fabric marker (optional)

Embroidery needle and stranded floss in dark green or dark brown

Felt and paper silk in assorted colors for leaves

Buttons for rosettes

Sewing needle and thread to match rosettes

Clothesline installed outdoors

Stones and clothespins (to hold the house in place)

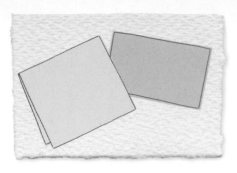

1 Work on a large, clean surface where you can spread out the fabric. Using a set square (or the corner of a large book or magazine), tape measure, long ruler, and pencil, mark out a 51 x 120in (1.3 x 3m) rectangle from the fabric for the walls and a 57 x 35in (145 x 90cm) rectangle from the roof fabric. Either fray the edges of the fabric (see Floral Wall Hanging, step 1, page 36) or press under and stitch a narrow hem—or use a combination of both, fraying some edges and hemming the others.

2 Fold the roof rectangle in half lengthwise and mark the fold with tailor's chalk. For the roof tiles, draw and cut out a U-shaped pattern that is 4¼in (11cm) wide and 4in (10cm) deep. Fold the white felt in half and cut around the pattern through both layers 16 times to make 32 felt tiles. Pin 16 tiles so their straight ends are just to one side of the marked central line on the fabric, and parallel to it. The tiles should overlap and extend for the full length of the roof rectangle. Machine stitch along the straight end of the tiles from one end of the roof fabric to the other. Repeat to attach the other tiles just the other side of the central line. Pin and machine stitch a length of rickrack near each long edge of this rectangle.

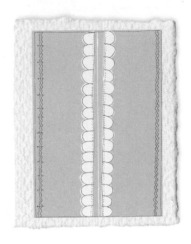

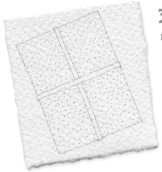

3 Cut out a 11 x 10in (28 x 25cm) rectangle for the pocket window. Iron fusible web to the wrong side of the fabrics for the remaining windows and door, and cut out rectangles for them. The door here is 20 x 13in (50 x 32cm) and the windows are a little smaller than the pocket window. I prefer the uneven look you get from cutting out freehand without a ruler. Make windowpanes on some windows by pinning two lengths of ribbon in a cross shape and folding the ends to the back of the window rectangles, then machine stitching in place. Or you could create panes with machine stitching, hand embroidery, or a fabric pen. For the pocket window, you could turn under and press a narrow hem on all four edges, machine stitching the hem on the top edge.

4 Fold the house rectangle in half crosswise and fold the roof rectangle in half along the line between the tiles. Lay them both on the work surface, with the roof in position, so you can see where to put the door and windows. Remove the backing paper, and pin the door and windows to the house fabric. Iron them in place, removing the pins as you go. Now remove the roof, unfold the house, and machine stitch around the edges

of the doors and windows. On the pocket window leave the top edge unstitched.

5 From the fabric you backed with fusible web, cut out additional features such as windowsills, house numbers, and a mailbox. Remove the backing paper and iron them in place on the house fabric—for the mailbox, iron only the top edge, to allow it to flap.

6 With tailor's chalk, draw on the wall the outline of a flowering plant growing up it. With an embroidery needle and all six strands of the dark green or dark brown floss, embroider a stem in running stitch. Cut out some leaves from the fabric with fusible web on the back, remove the backing, and iron these leaves in place on the stem. Also cut out some more leaves from felt and paper silk (with no fusible web on the back), and attach these using the same floss in running stitch down the middle or around the edge of each.

7 For flowers, hand sew running stitch along one long edge of 8in (20cm) lengths of ribbon and pull up these threads to gather the ribbons into rosettes. Knot the threads at the back and sew a button in the center of each, then sew these onto the stem.

8 To put up the playhouse, first make sure the clothesline is at a height that will allow the walls to reach the ground when they are in a tent shape. Drape the house over the clothesline and use stones at the corners to hold it in place. Place the roof on top, and fasten both layers with clothespins.

Animal tracks
picnic blanket

This picnic blanket is not only more fun than traditional ones, it's also more practical, because it is has a waterproof underside and it is lighter and less bulky. It folds up small enough to pop into your picnic basket or it can be kept in its own small cotton tote. The animal tracks are stenciled—either use the ones I've chosen, for which there are patterns, or devise your own. To teach children about the local wildlife, you could show the tracks of animals found near your home or let your imagination run wild with Bigfoot or dinosaur tracks. One little creature like a duck could be walking next to a large one such as a bear, and the tracks could meander off and on the blanket.

materials and equipment

Prewashed cream fabric, such as a polycotton, that will not shrink or crease in washing

Lightweight waterproof fabric

Set square (or large magazine or book), tape measure, and long ruler

Pencil

Dressmaker's shears and small, sharp scissors

Patterns for tracks (see page 184)

Scrap paper

Frisket masking film in matte finish

Cutting mat and craft knife

Large piece of plastic sheeting (optional)

Stencil brush or stiff flat paintbrush, ½in (1.5cm) wide

Thick fabric paint such as Marabu-Textil Plus (which can be washed in the washing machine up to 100°F/40°C)

Paper towel or tissue

Sponge

Pins

Sewing machine and thread to match fabric

Iron and ironing board

Small cotton tote, measuring about 14 x 17in (35 x 43cm) (optional)

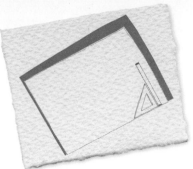

1 Place the cream fabric on top of the waterproof fabric, wrong sides together, with the selvages even. Using a set square (or the corner of a magazine or large book), a long ruler, and a pencil, mark out a 48 x 57in (120 x 145cm) rectangle. Cut out with dressmaker's shears.

2 Using patterns you have made yourself or the patterns in this book, plan your design on some scrap paper. Decide what groupings of prints could form a stencil—for some of the prints I used a combination of four prints on one stencil, while for others I used just two prints on one stencil. Now draw around the patterns onto the Frisket film (see Tip, page 93) to make the stencils. Place them on a cutting mat and cut out with a craft knife.

3 If you have a piece of plastic sheeting larger than the rectangle, lay the cream fabric, flat and right side up, on top of it. If you don't have any large sheeting, then lay the cream fabric on top of the waterproof fabric (still with wrong sides together) on your work surface.

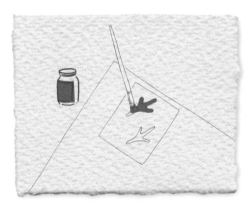

Beginning at the top of the design, position the stencil for your first print, sticky side down, on the right side of the cream fabric, and smooth down the edges of the stencil. Load the stencil brush or stiff flat brush with some paint—don't overload it or the paint will seep under the edges. Now, holding the brush at right angles to the fabric and using a dabbing action, stipple the paint onto the fabric through the window in the stencil until you have covered the entire cut-out shape right up to the edges.

4 Peel off the stencil (it doesn't have to be completely dry). If there has been some seepage under the edge, wipe the paint off the stencil using a paper towel or tissue. Place the stencil in the next position, leaving an appropriate gap, and repeat step 3. Continue until you have completed the design. Where two "trails" meet, avoid overlapping the tracks, or it could just look muddled—instead, simply continue the new trail on the other side of the old one.

5 When the paint is dry, peel the cream fabric away from the plastic sheeting or the waterproof fabric. If you have used the latter, wipe over it with a damp sponge to remove any paint that has seeped through, and leave to dry—as it will be hidden, don't worry too much if you can't get it completely clean.

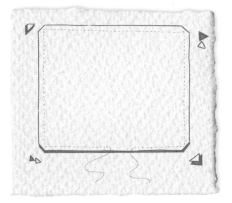

6 Pin the two layers of fabric with right sides together. Machine stitch a 1in (2.5cm) seam around all four edges, pivoting at the corners (see Reversible Collar Neckpiece, Tip, page 137) and leaving a 12in (30cm) opening in the bottom edge. Snip off the corners of the seam allowance.

7 Turn right side out, and slipstitch the opening closed as shown. Press with the iron set at a low temperature.

8 If you have a tote to keep the blanket in, you could stencil some tracks on it to match, but be sure to place some plain scrap paper (not newspaper) inside it first to absorb any paint that seeps through.

Decorated
chair and stool

I bought this little wooden child's chair and stool at a flea market. They looked tired and shabby but were easily transformed into children's seating that is perfect for the garden. I started by painting them white all over, and then because each slat creates a natural stripe, I painted some of the slats in different colors to match the vintage chintz fabric that I pasted onto the remaining slats. I then distressed the paintwork a little to add to the soft, faded look, and I finished with a protective coat of varnish. If you can't find an old chair and stool for this project, the same technique could be used to spruce up a new plain wooden chair, or a new slatted wooden stool.

materials and equipment

Old chair and stool with slats

Fine sandpaper and sponge

Undercoat

1¼in (3cm) and ½in (1.5cm) flat paintbrushes

Flat latex (emulsion) or latex velvet (vinyl silk) paint in white

Acrylic paints or tester pots of latex (emulsion) paint in three colors to match fabric

Three glass jars with lids, for mixing paints (optional)

Ruler and tailor's chalk

Floral fabric

Dressmaker's shears

White glue

Clear-drying flat varnish and brush

1 Lightly sand the chair and stool if necessary, and then wipe them down with a damp sponge. When dry, apply an undercoat using a 1¼in (3cm) flat brush. Try not to create any runs of paint. When the paint is dry, turn the chair and stool upside down and paint the remaining parts. When dry, rub down any paint runs with sandpaper and paint with a white top coat. Leave to dry.

2 If you are mixing your own acrylic colors, mix enough of each to apply two coats to the tops of the seat slats and the fronts of the back slats. Whether using these, or premixed acrylics, or tester pots of latex (emulsion), decide where you will use each color. Aim to have a different color for each painted chair-seat slat, leaving some of the slats to be covered with fabric instead, and then you could repeat the colors/fabric on the chair back and the stool. Using a ½in (1.5cm) flat brush, paint each slat in its chosen color, being careful to paint only up to the edge of the slat, without going over it onto the side of the slat. Leave to dry, and then apply a second coat.

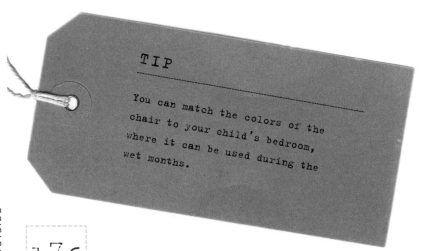

TIP

You can match the colors of the chair to your child's bedroom, where it can be used during the wet months.

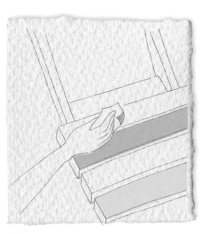

3 When dry, lightly sand some areas to give a pleasingly worn, distressed look.

4 Measure the tops of the remaining slats, and mark their size and shape on your fabric using tailor's chalk, taking into account the position of the fabric's pattern. Cut out the pieces. Generously apply white glue to one of these slats, taking it right up to the edges. Place the fabric piece on top, sliding it around while the glue is still wet, until the edges are even. If necessary, trim off any excess fabric. Repeat for the other pieces of fabric.

5 When the glue has dried, varnish the surface of the fabric and the painted slats to seal them and make them more durable.

QUICK IDEAS
Fruit crates for plants

The wooden crates you see in fruit and vegetable markets often have pretty color pictures printed on the sides, and I love the contrast of the dainty images with the rough wood and slight crookedness of the boxes. It's easy to turn these crates into charming containers in which children can grow a crop of small plants, fruit, or vegetables.

✳ Obtain some crates from a market stall (with the stallholder's permission, of course!) and carefully paint around the images using a household paint—I chose a blue-gray water-based eggshell paint— and a small artist's brush. Then use a flat brush to apply this paint to the remainder of each box.

✳ If the base of a crate is solid, drill a few drainage holes in it. Line the boxes with burlap (hessian), or with plastic in which you have cut drainage holes.

✳ Fill the crates with soil and plant with vegetable, herb, or flower seeds. Children will enjoy helping with this, and they can then water and care for the seedlings and eat their produce.

Alphabet pebbles

This is a great project in which to involve children. Scour the beach for a good selection of smooth, flat, regular pebbles, or, if you don't live near the coast, buy a bag of them from a garden center. You'll need enough for a full alphabet, which children could practice putting in the right order or use for games of I Spy. And if you make extra alphabet pebbles with the most common vowels and consonants, and perhaps capital letters, they could also be used for word games. Once the alphabet pebbles are completed, they can be stacked or stored in drawstring bags or shoeboxes. Don't leave them outdoors for long in wet weather in case they become unreadable.

✺ The Alphabet Pebbles are easy to make. Wash them first in warm, soapy water and leave to dry thoroughly. Meanwhile, go through old magazines and carefully cut out all the letters you will need.

✺ Use a small paintbrush to apply clear-drying glue such as white glue onto the underside of each letter, and then stick the letter in place. Paint more glue over the top of the letter, taking the glue over the edge of the paper onto the stone to stop the letter from peeling off. In fact, you could paint the whole pebble with the glue to seal it—or wait for the glued-on letters to dry and then apply a clear flat varnish over the entire pebble, which will bring out the color of the stones and lend a slight sheen.

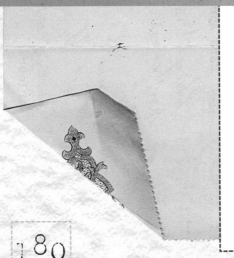

Twirling
ribbon sticks

In devising these I had a vision of my children dancing around the garden with the ribbon sticks creating flashes of swirling color in midair behind them, against the green of the garden or a dark, dramatic wall. A stick with a single ribbon is the most effective for twirling, leaving a lovely swishy trail of color, but multiple ribbons in zingy color combinations on a stick will twist and twirl around themselves and are perfect for dancing around with and playing with friends.

✺ Rummage through your ribbon box or have fun in a notions (haberdashery) department choosing ribbons that look good together, such as reds with pinks, lime green with blues, yellows with turquoise. Be sure to think at the same time about the color you'll paint the stick.

✺ With a saw, cut ⅜in (8–10mm) wooden dowels to a length of about 18in (45cm) for young children or about 25in (65cm) for older children. Sand the ends and paint the sticks with a household paint such as acrylic. Lean it against a tub of paint to dry, and then give it a quick second coat and leave to dry.

✺ Cut the ribbon(s) to a length of about 33–78in (83–200cm). For the multi-ribbon sticks, I used four or five ribbons, with one longer than the rest: about 55in (140cm). Mark a point 1¼–1½in (3–4cm) from the top of the stick and apply a strong all-purpose glue to this part of the stick. Stick a ribbon to it with the end of the ribbon even with the mark. If using more than one ribbon on the stick, glue the ends of the remaining ribbons in place in the same way, spacing them evenly around the stick and overlapping them if necessary. Leave to dry.

✺ Cut a 4in (10cm) length of ribbon and stick some double-sided tape to the wrong side. Remove the backing from the tape and wrap the ribbon tightly around the stick three times, covering the glued end(s) of the ribbon(s).

Templates

Make a pattern by photocopying the template to the same size or enlarging it, as directed on each template. Some templates overlap but you can tell them apart by the colors.

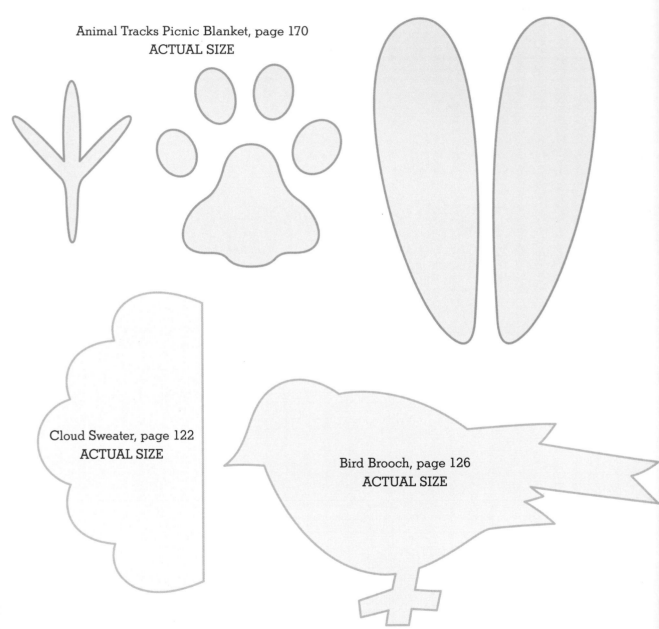

Animal Tracks Picnic Blanket, page 170
ACTUAL SIZE

Cloud Sweater, page 122
ACTUAL SIZE

Bird Brooch, page 126
ACTUAL SIZE

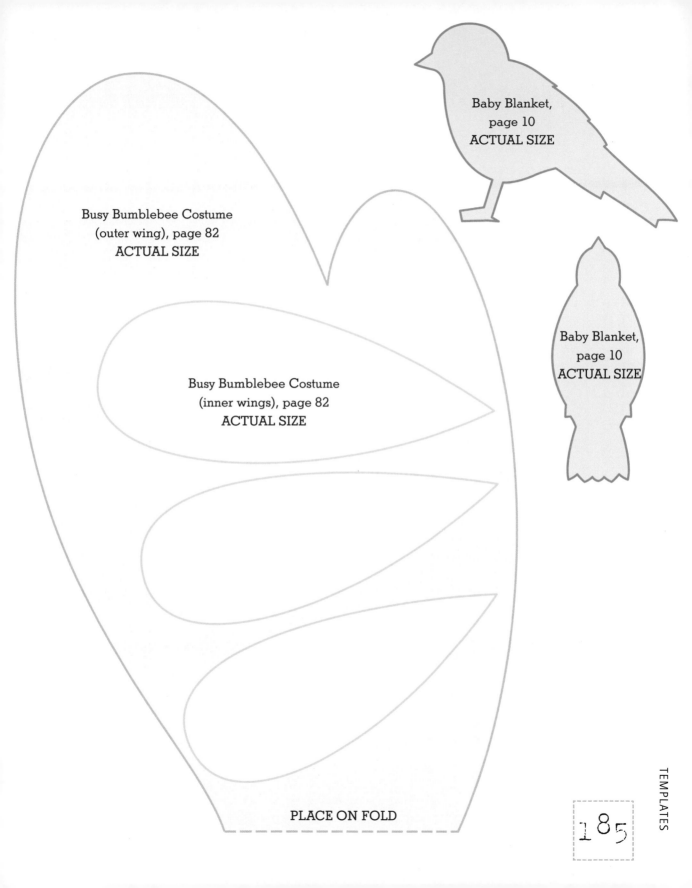

Baby Blanket,
page 10
ACTUAL SIZE

Busy Bumblebee Costume
(outer wing), page 82
ACTUAL SIZE

Busy Bumblebee Costume
(inner wings), page 82
ACTUAL SIZE

Baby Blanket,
page 10
ACTUAL SIZE

PLACE ON FOLD

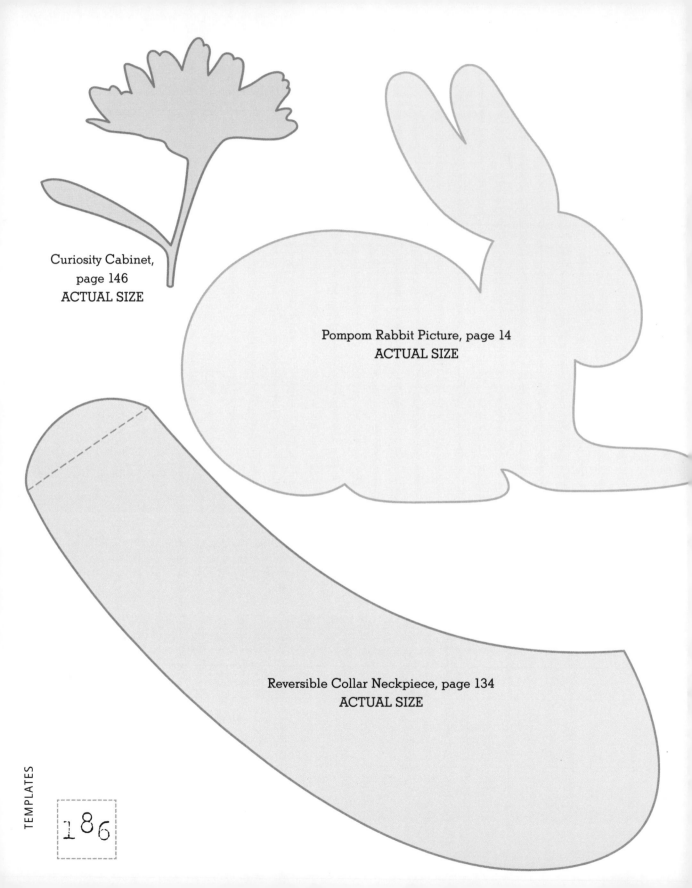

Curiosity Cabinet,
page 146
ACTUAL SIZE

Pompom Rabbit Picture, page 14
ACTUAL SIZE

Reversible Collar Neckpiece, page 134
ACTUAL SIZE

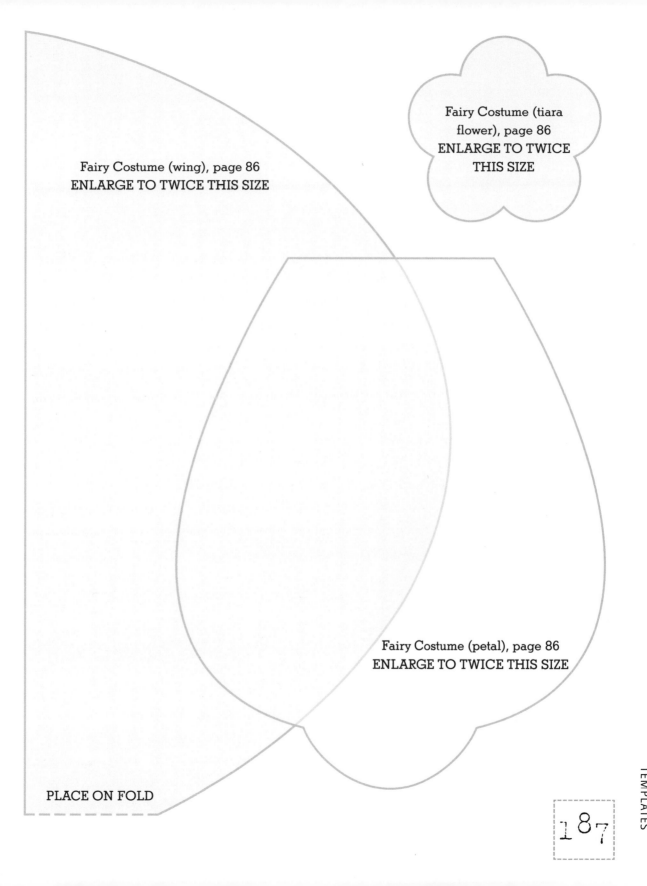

Fairy Costume (wing), page 86
ENLARGE TO TWICE THIS SIZE

Fairy Costume (tiara flower), page 86
ENLARGE TO TWICE THIS SIZE

Fairy Costume (petal), page 86
ENLARGE TO TWICE THIS SIZE

PLACE ON FOLD

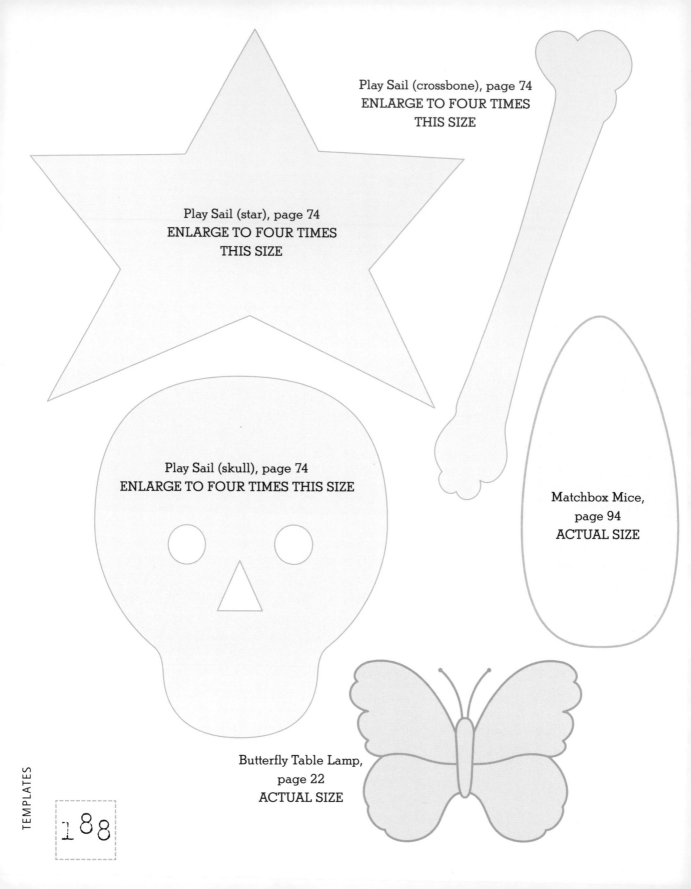

Play Sail (crossbone), page 74
ENLARGE TO FOUR TIMES
THIS SIZE

Play Sail (star), page 74
ENLARGE TO FOUR TIMES
THIS SIZE

Play Sail (skull), page 74
ENLARGE TO FOUR TIMES THIS SIZE

Matchbox Mice,
page 94
ACTUAL SIZE

Butterfly Table Lamp,
page 22
ACTUAL SIZE

TEMPLATES

188

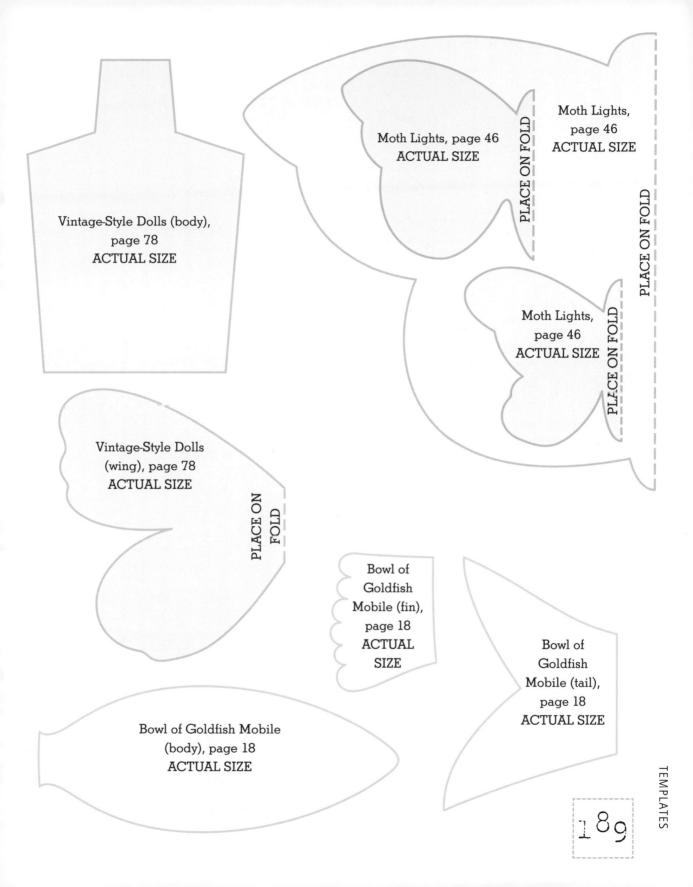

Vintage-Style Dolls (body),
page 78
ACTUAL SIZE

Moth Lights, page 46
ACTUAL SIZE

Moth Lights,
page 46
ACTUAL SIZE

PLACE ON FOLD

Moth Lights,
page 46
ACTUAL SIZE

PLACE ON FOLD

PLACE ON FOLD

Vintage-Style Dolls
(wing), page 78
ACTUAL SIZE

PLACE ON FOLD

Bowl of
Goldfish
Mobile (fin),
page 18
ACTUAL
SIZE

Bowl of
Goldfish
Mobile (tail),
page 18
ACTUAL SIZE

Bowl of Goldfish Mobile
(body), page 18
ACTUAL SIZE

Sailboat-at-Anchor Bed Runner (hull),
page 38
ENLARGE TO FOUR TIMES THIS SIZE

Sailboat-at-Anchor Bed Runner
(anchor), page 38
ENLARGE TO FOUR TIMES
THIS SIZE

Sailboat-at-Anchor Bed Runner
(mainsail), page 38
ENLARGE TO FOUR TIMES
THIS SIZE

Sailboat-at-Anchor
Bed Runner
(triangular sails),
page 38
ENLARGE TO FOUR
TIMES THIS SIZE

Sailboat-at-Anchor Bed Runner (flag), page 38
ACTUAL SIZE

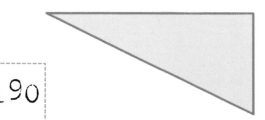

Index

Acknowledgments
A huge, heartfelt thank you to everyone who bought my first book, *The Homemade Home*, for the wonderful feedback I have received and to the lovely friends I have made along the way.

Thank you to everyone at CICO Books for giving me the opportunity to write another book and for your valuable input and help. To Emma Lee for the beautiful photographs and making our shoot days fun and to Polly Ord for your generous dedication of time and assistance. To Caramel Baby & Child for your kind loans of the most wonderful children's clothes and to V V Rouleaux—the best ribbon shop in the world in my opinion.

To my children, who were the inspiration behind this book, for their feedback when I was coming up with ideas for projects and their delight when I created something they loved. Thank you for letting me use your drawings. Thank you to my lovely husband for his patience, understanding, and support. I made this book for all of you.

About the author:
Sania Pell is an author, interiors stylist, and designer, known for bringing a unique, handmade aspect to her work for publications such as *Elle Decoration*, *The Sunday Telegraph*, and *The Mail on Sunday*. After studying textile design at Edinburgh College of Art, Sania worked for one of London's top textile design studios for seven years. During this time she gained valuable commercial experience designing for different markets including Europe, the US, and Japan. Wanting a new challenge, she retrained as an interior stylist. Her first book, *The Homemade Home*, was published by CICO Books in 2009. Sania lives in London with her husband and two young children. Her blog can be found at:
www.saniapell.com/athomeblog